Holy Sweet!:

300 Recipes for Bigger, and Better Desserts

Donna D. Thornton

BAKED LEMON PUDDING. (Queen of Puddings.)

Ingredients.—One quart of milk, two cupfuls of bread crumbs, four eggs, whites and yolks beaten separately, butter the size of an egg, one cupful of white sugar, one large lemon—juice and grated rind. Heat the milk and pour over the bread crumbs, add the butter, cover and let it get soft. When cool, beat the sugar and yolks and add to the mixture, also the grated rind. Bake in a buttered dish until firm and slightly brown, from a half to three-quarters of an hour. When done, draw it to the door of the oven and cover with a meringue made of the whites of the eggs, whipped to a froth with four tablespoonfuls of powdered sugar and the lemon juice; put it back in the oven and brown a light straw color. Eat warm, with lemon sauce.

LEMON PUDDING.

A small cupful of butter, the grated peel of two large lemons and the juice of one, the yolks of ten eggs and whites of five, a cupful and a half of white sugar. Beat all together and, lining a deep pudding-dish with puff paste, bake the lemon pudding in it; while baking, beat the whites of the remaining five eggs to a stiff froth, whip in fine white sugar to taste, cover the top of the pudding (when baked) with the meringue and return to the oven for a moment to brown; eat cold, it requires no sauce.

BOILED LEMON PUDDING.

Half a cupful of chopped suet, one pint of bread crumbs, one lemon, one cupful of sugar, one of flour, a teaspoonful of salt and two eggs, milk. First mix the suet, bread crumbs, sugar and flour well together, adding the lemon peel, which should be the yellow grated from the outside, and the juice, which should be strained. When these ingredients are well mixed, moisten with the eggs and sufficient milk to make the pudding of the consistency of thick batter; put it into a well-buttered mold and boil for three and a half hours; turn it out, strew sifted sugar over and serve warm with the lemon sauce, or not, at pleasure.

LEMON PUDDING, COLD.

One cupful of sugar, four eggs, the whites and yolks beaten separately, two tablespoonfuls of cornstarch, one pint of milk, one tablespoonful of butter and the juice and rind of two lemons. Wet the cornstarch in some of the milk, then stir it into the remainder of the milk, which should be boiling on the stove, stirring constantly and briskly for five minutes. Take it from the stove, stir in the butter and let it cool. Beat the yolks and sugar together, then stir them thoroughly into the milk and cornstarch. Now stir in the lemon juice and grated rind, doing it very gradually, making it very smooth. Bake in a well-buttered dish. To be eaten cold. Oranges may be used in place of lemons. This also may be turned while *hot* into several small cups or forms previously dipped in cold water, place them aside; in one hour they will be fit to turn out. Serve with cream and sugar. Should be boiled altogether, not baked.

ROYAL SAGO PUDDING.

Three-quarters of a cupful of sago washed and put into one quart of milk; put it into a saucepan, let it stand in boiling water on the stove or range until the sago has well swelled. While hot, put in two tablespoonfuls of butter with one cupful of white sugar and flavoring. When cool, add the well-beaten yolks of four eggs, put in a buttered pudding-dish, and bake from half to three-quarters of an hour; then remove it from the oven and place it to cool. Beat the whites of the eggs with three tablespoonfuls of powdered white sugar till they are a mass of froth; spread the pudding with either raspberry or strawberry jam, and then spread on the frosting; put in the oven for two minutes to slightly brown. If made in summer, be sure and keep the whites of the eggs on ice until ready for use and beat them in the coolest place you can find, as it will make a much richer frosting.

The small white sago called pearl is the best. The large brown kind has an earthy taste. It should always be kept in a covered jar or box.

This pudding, made with tapioca, is equally as good. Serve with any sweet sauce.

SAGO APPLE PUDDING.

One cupful of sago in a quart of tepid water, with a pinch of salt, soaked for one hour; six or eight apples pared and cored, or quartered, and steamed tender and put in the pudding-dish; boil and stir the sago until clear, adding water to make it thin, and pour it over the apples; bake one hour. This is good hot, with butter and sugar, or cold with cream and sugar.

PLAIN SAGO PUDDING.

Make the same as TAPIOCA PUDDING, substituting sago for tapioca.

CHOCOLATE PUDDING. No. 1.

Make cornstarch pudding with a quart of milk, three tablespoonfuls of cornstarch and three tablespoonfuls of sugar. When done, remove about half and flavor to taste, and then to that remaining in the kettle add an egg beaten very light, and four tablespoonfuls of vanilla chocolate grated and dissolved in a little milk. Put in a mold, alternately the dark and light. Serve with whipped cream or boiled custard. This is more of a blanc mange than a pudding.

CHOCOLATE PUDDING. No. 2.

One quart of sweet milk, three-quarters of a cupful of grated chocolate; scald the milk and chocolate together; when *cool*, add the yolks of five eggs, one cupful of sugar; flavor with vanilla. Bake about twenty-five minutes. Beat the five whites of eggs to a stiff froth, adding four tablespoonfuls of fine sugar, spread evenly over the top and brown slightly in the oven.

CHOCOLATE PUDDING. No. 3.

One quart of milk, fourteen even tablespoonfuls of grated bread crumbs, twelve tablespoonfuls grated chocolate, six eggs, one tablespoonful vanilla, sugar to make very sweet. Separate the yolks and whites of four eggs, beat up the four yolks and two whole eggs together very light with the sugar. Put the milk on the range, and when it come to a perfect boil pour it over the bread and chocolate; add the beaten eggs and sugar and vanilla; be sure it is sweet enough; pour into a buttered dish; bake one hour in a moderate oven. When cold, and just before it is served, have the four whites beaten with a little powdered-sugar and flavor with vanilla and use as a meringue.

CHOCOLATE PUDDING. No. 4.

Half a cake of chocolate broken in one quart of milk and put on the range until it reaches boiling point; remove the mixture from the range; add four teaspoonfuls of cornstarch mixed with the yolks of three eggs and one cup and a half of sugar; stir constantly until thick; remove from the fire and flavor with vanilla; pour the mixture in a dish; beat the whites of the three eggs to a stiff froth and add a little sugar; cover the top of the pudding with a meringue and set in the oven until a light brown. Serve cold.

TAPIOCA PUDDING.

Five tablespoonfuls of tapioca, one quart of milk, two ounces of butter, a cupful of sugar, four eggs, flavoring of vanilla or bitter almonds. Wash the tapioca and let it stew gently in the milk on the back part of the stove for a quarter of an hour, occasionally stirring it; then let it cool, mix with it the butter, sugar and eggs, which should be well-beaten, and flavor with either of the above ingredients. Butter a dish, put in the pudding and bake in a moderate oven for an hour. If the pudding is boiled, add a little more tapioca and boil it in a buttered basin one and a half hours.

STRAWBERRY TAPIOCA.

This makes a most delightful dessert. Soak over night a large teacupful of tapioca in cold water; in the morning, put half of it in a buttered yellow-ware baking-dish, or any suitable pudding-dish. Sprinkle sugar over the tapioca; then on this put a quart of berries, sugar and the rest of the tapioca. Fill the dish with water, which should cover the tapioca about a quarter of an inch. Bake in a moderately hot oven until it looks clear. Eat cold with cream or Custard. If not sweet enough, add more sugar at table; and in baking, if it seems too dry, more water is needed.

A similar dish may be made, using peaches, either fresh or canned.

RASPBERRY PUDDING.

One-quarter cup of butter, one-half cupful of sugar, two cupfuls of jam, six cupfuls of soft bread crumbs, four eggs. Rub the butter and sugar together, beat the eggs, yolks and whites separately, mash the raspberries, add the whites beaten to a stiff froth, stir all together to a smooth paste; butter a pudding dish, cover the bottom with a layer of the crumbs, then a layer of the mixture; continue the alternate layers until the dish is full, making the last layer of crumbs; bake one hour in a moderate oven. Serve in the dish in which it is baked and serve with fruit sauce made with raspberries. This pudding may be made the same with any other kind of berries.

PEAR, PEACH AND APPLE PUDDING.

Pare some nice ripe pears (to weigh about three-fourths of a pound); put them in a saucepan with a few cloves, some lemon or orange peel, and stew about a quarter of an hour in two cupfuls of water; put them in your pudding-dish, and having made the following custard, one pint of cream or milk, four eggs, sugar to taste, a pinch of salt and a tablespoonful of flour; beat eggs and sugar well, add the flour, grate some nutmeg, add the cream by degrees, stirring all the time,—pour this over the pears and bake in a *quick* oven. Apples or peaches may be substituted.

Serve cold with sweetened cream.

FIG PUDDINGS.

Half a pound of good dried figs, washed, wiped and minced, two cupfuls of fine, dry bread crumbs, three eggs, half a cupful of beef suet, powdered, two scant cupfuls of sweet milk, half a cupful of white sugar, a little salt, half a teaspoonful of baking powder, stirred in half a cupful of sifted flour. Soak the crumbs in milk, add the eggs, beaten light, with sugar, salt, suet, flour and figs. Beat three minutes, put in buttered molds with tight top, set in boiling water with weight on cover to prevent mold from upsetting, and boil three hours. Eat hot with hard sauce or butter, powdered sugar, one teaspoonful of extract of nutmeg.

FRUIT PUDDING, CORN MEAL.

Take a pint of hot milk and stir in sifted Indian meal till the batter is stiff; add a teaspoonful of salt and half a cup of molasses, adding a teaspoonful of soda dissolved; then stir in a pint of whortleberries or chopped sweet apple; tie in a cloth that has been wet, and leave room for it to swell, or put in a pudding-pan and tie a cloth over; boil three hours; the water must boil when it is put in; you can use cranberries and sweet sauce.

APPLE CORN MEAL PUDDING.

Pare and core twelve pippin apples; slice them very thin; then stir into one quart of new milk one quart of sifted corn meal; add a little salt, then the apples, four spoonfuls of chopped suet and a teacupful of good molasses, adding a teaspoonful of soda dissolved; mix these well together, pour into a buttered dish and bake four hours; serve hot with sugar and wine sauce. This is the most simple, cheap and luxuriant fruit pudding that can be made.

RHUBARB OR PIE-PLANT PUDDING.

Chop rhubarb pretty fine, put in a pudding dish and sprinkle sugar over it; make a batter of one cupful of sour milk, two eggs, a piece of butter the size of an egg, half a teaspoonful of soda and enough flour to make batter about as thick as for cake. Spread it over the rhubarb and bake till done. Turn out on a platter upside down, so that the rhubarb will be on top. Serve with sugar and cream.

FRUIT PUDDINGS.

Fruit puddings, such as green gooseberry, are very nice made in a basin, the basin to be buttered and lined with a paste, rolling it round to the thickness of half an inch; then get a pint of gooseberries and three ounces of sugar; after having made your paste, take half the fruit and lay it at the bottom of your basin; then add half your sugar, then put the remainder of the gooseberries in and the remainder of the sugar; on that, draw your paste to the centre, join the edges well together, put the cloth over the whole, tying it at the bottom, and boil in plenty of water. Fruit puddings of this kind, such as apples and rhubarb, should be done in this manner.

Boil for an hour, take out of the saucepan, untie the cloth, turn out on a dish, or let it remain in the basin and serve with sugar over.

A thin cover of the paste may be rolled round and put over the pudding.

Ripe cherries, currants, raspberries, greengages, plums and such like fruit, will not require so much sugar, or so long boiling. These puddings are also very good steamed.

SNOW PUDDING.

One-half a package Cox's gelatine; pour over it a cupful of cold water and add one and a half cupfuls of sugar; when 'soft, add one cupful of boiling water and the juice of one lemon; then the whites of four well-beaten eggs; beat all together until it is light and frothy, or until the gelatine will not settle clear in the bottom of the dish after standing a few minutes; put it on a glass dish. Serve with a custard made of one pint of milk, the yolks of four eggs, four tablespoonfuls of sugar and the grated rind of a lemon; boil.

DELMONICO PUDDING.

Three tablespoonfuls of cornstarch, the yolks of five eggs, six tablespoonfuls of sugar; beat the eggs light, then add the sugar and beat again till very light; mix the cornstarch with a little cold milk; mix all together and stir into one quart of milk just as it is about to boil, having added a little salt; stir it until it has thickened well; pour it into a dish for the table and place it in the oven until it will bear icing; place over the top a layer of canned peaches or other fruit (and it improves it to mix the syrup of the fruit with the custard part); beat the whites to a stiff froth with two tablespoonfuls of white sugar to an egg; then put it into the oven until it is a light brown.

This is a very delicate and delicious pudding.

SAUCER PUDDINGS.

Two tablespoonfuls of flour, two tablespoonfuls of powdered sugar, three eggs, a teacupful of milk, butter, preserve of any kind. Mix the flour and sugar, beat the eggs, add them to the milk, and beat up with the flour and sugar. Butter well three saucers, half fill them, and bake in a quick oven about twenty minutes. Remove them from the saucers when cool enough, cut in half, and spread a thin layer of preserves between each half; close them again, and serve with cream.

NANTUCKET PUDDING.

One quart of berries or any small fruit, two tablespoonfuls of flour, two tablespoonfuls of sugar; simmer together and turn into molds; cover with frosting as for cake, or with whipped eggs and sugar, browning lightly in the oven; serve with cream.

TOAST PUDDING.

Toast several thin slices of stale bread, removing the crust, butter them well, and pour over them hot stewed fruit in alternate layers. Serve warm with rich hot sauce.

PLAIN RICE PUDDING.

Pick over, wash and boil, a teacupful of rice; when soft drain off the water; while warm, add to it a tablespoonful of cold butter. When cool, mix with it a cupful of sugar, a teaspoonful of grated nutmeg and one of ground cinnamon. Beat up four eggs very light, whites and yolks separately; add them to the rice; then stir in a quart of sweet milk gradually. Butter a pudding-dish, turn in the mixture and bake one hour in a moderate oven. Serve warm, with sweet wine sauce.

If you have cold cooked rice, first soak it in the milk and proceed as above.

RICE PUDDING. (Fine.)

Wash a teacupful of rice and boil it in two teacupfuls of water; then add, while the rice is hot, three tablespoonfuls of butter, five tablespoonful of sugar, five eggs well beaten, one tablespoonful of powdered nutmeg, a little salt, one glass of wine, a, quarter of a pound of raisins, stoned and cut in halves, a quarter of a pound of Zante currants, a quarter of a pound of citron cut in slips, and one quart of cream; mix well, pour into a buttered dish and bake an hour in a moderate oven.

Astor House, New York City.

RICE MERINGUE.

One cupful of carefully sorted rice boiled in water until it is soft; when done, drain it so as to remove all the water; cool it, and add one quart of new milk, the well-beaten yolks of three eggs, three tablespoonfuls of white sugar and a little nutmeg, or flavor with lemon or vanilla; pour into a baking dish and bake about half an hour. Let it get cold; beat the whites of the eggs, add two tablespoonfuls of sugar, flavor with lemon or vanilla; drop or spread it over the pudding and slightly brown it in the oven.

RICE LEMON PUDDING.

Put on to boil one quart of milk, and when it simmers stir in four tablespoonfuls of rice flour that has been moistened in a little milk; let it come to a boil and remove from the fire; add one quarter of a pound of butter, and, when cool, the grated peel with the juice of two lemons, and the yolks and beaten whites of four eggs; sweeten to taste; one wine-glassful of wine, put in the last thing, is also an improvement.

RICE PUDDING WITHOUT EGGS.

Two quarts of milk, two-thirds of a cupful of rice, a cupful of sugar, a piece of butter as large as a walnut, a teaspoonful of cinnamon, a little nutmeg and a pinch of salt. Put into a deep pudding-dish, well buttered, set into a moderate oven; stir it once or twice until it begins to cook, let it remain in the oven about two hours (until it is the consistency of cream). Eat cold.

FRUIT RICE PUDDING.

One large teacupful of rice, a little water to cook it partially; dry, line an earthen basin with part of it; fill nearly full with pared, cored and quartered apples, or any fruit you choose; cover with the balance of your rice; tie a cloth tightly over the top and steam one hour. To be eaten with sweet sauce. Do not butter your dish.

BOILED RICE PUDDING. No. 1.

One cupful of cold boiled rice, one cupful of sugar, four eggs, a pinch of soda and a pinch of salt. Put it all in a bowl and beat it up until it is very light and white. Beat four ounces of butter to a cream, put it into the pudding and ten drops of essence of lemon. Beat altogether for five minutes. Butter a mold, pour the pudding into it and boil for two hours. Serve with sweet fruit sauce.

BOILED RICE PUDDING. No. 2.

Wash two teacupfuls of rice and soak it in water for half an hour; then turn off the water and mix the rice with half a pound of raisins stoned and cut in halves; add a little salt, tie the whole in a cloth, leaving room for the rice to swell to twice its natural size, and boil two hours in plenty of water; serve with wine sauce.

RICE SNOW-BALLS.

Wash two teacupfuls of rice and boil it in one teacupful of water and one of milk, with a little salt; if the rice is not tender when the milk and water are absorbed, add a little more milk and water; when the rice is tender, flavor with vanilla, form it into balls, or mold it into a compact form with little cups; place these rice balls around the inside of a deep dish, fill the dish with a rich soft custard and serve either hot or cold. The custard and balls should be flavored with the same.

PRUNE PUDDING.

Heat a little more than a pint of sweet milk to the boiling point, then stir in gradually a little cold milk in which you have rubbed smooth a heaping tablespoonful of cornstarch; add sugar to suit your taste, three well-beaten eggs, about a teaspoonful of butter and a little grated nutmeg. Let this come to a boil, then pour it in a buttered pudding-dish, first adding a cupful of stewed prunes, with the stones taken out. Bake for from fifteen to twenty minutes, according to the state of the oven. Serve with or without sauce. A little cream improves it if poured over it when placed in saucers.

BLACKBERRY OR WHORTLEBERRY PUDDING.

Three cupfuls of flour, one cupful of molasses, half a cupful of milk, a teaspoonful of salt, a little cloves and cinnamon, a teaspoonful of soda dissolved in a little of the milk. Stir in a quart of huckleberries, floured. Boil in a well-buttered mold two hours. Serve with brandy sauce.

BAKED HUCKLEBERRY PUDDING.

One quart of ripe fresh huckleberries or blueberries, half a teaspoonful of mace or nutmeg, three eggs, well beaten, separately, two cupfuls of sugar, one tablespoonful of cold butter, one cupful of sweet milk, one pint of flour, two teaspoonfuls of baking powder. Roll the berries well in the flour and add them last of all. Bake half an hour and serve with sauce. There is no more delicate and delicious pudding than this.

FRUIT PUDDING.

This pudding is made without cooking and is nice prepared the day before using.

Stew currants or any small fruits, either fresh or dried, sweeten with sugar to taste and pour hot over *thin* slices of bread with the crust cut off, placed in a suitable dish, first a layer of bread, then the hot stewed fruit, then bread and fruit, then bread, leaving the fruit last. Put a plate over the top and, when cool, set it on ice. Serve with sugar and cream.

This pudding is very fine made with Boston crackers split open and placed in layers with stewed peaches.

BOILED CURRANT PUDDING.

Five cupfuls of sifted flour in which two teaspoonfuls of baking powder have been sifted, one-half a cupful of chopped suet, half a pound of currants, milk, a pinch of salt. Wash the currants, dry them thoroughly and pick away any stalks or grit; chop the suet finely; mix all the ingredients together and moisten with sufficient milk to make the pudding into a stiff batter; tie it up in a floured cloth, put it into boiling water and boil for three hours and a half. Serve with jelly sauce made very sweet.

TRANSPARENT PUDDING.

A small cupful of fresh butter warmed, but not melted, one cupful of sifted sugar creamed with the butter, a teaspoonful of nutmeg, grated, eight eggs, yolks and whites beaten separately. Beat the butter and sugar light and then add the nutmeg and the beaten eggs, which should be stirred in gradually; flavor with vanilla, almond, peach or rose-water; stir *hard*; butter a deep dish, line with puff paste and bake half an hour. Then make a meringue for the top and brown. Serve cold.

SWEET-POTATO PUDDING.

To a large sweet potato, weighing two pounds, allow half a pound of sugar, half a pound of butter, one gill of sweet cream, one gill of strong wine or brandy, one grated nutmeg, a little lemon peel and four eggs. Boil the potato until thoroughly done, mash up fine, and while hot add the sugar and butter. Set aside to cool while you beat the eggs light and add the seasoning last. Line tin plates with puff paste, and pour in the mixture, bake in a moderate but regularly heated oven. When the puddings are drawn from the fire, cover the top with thinly-sliced bits of preserved citron or quince marmalade. Strew the top thickly with granulated white sugar and serve, with the addition of a glass of rich milk for each person at table.

PINEAPPLE PUDDING.

Butter a pudding-dish and line the bottom and sides with slices of stale cake (sponge cake is best); pare and slice thin a large pineapple, place in the dish first a layer of pineapple, then strew with sugar, then more pineapple, and so on until all is used. Pour over a small teacupful of water and cover with slices of cake which have been dipped in cold water; cover the whole with a buttered plate and bake slowly for two hours.

ORANGE ROLEY POLEY.

Make a light dough the same as for apple dumplings, roll it out into a long narrow sheet, about quarter of an inch thick. Spread thickly over it peeled and sliced oranges, sprinkle it plentifully with white sugar, scatter over all a teaspoonful or two of grated orange peel, then roll it up. Fold the edges well together to keep the juices from running out. Boil it in a floured cloth one hour and a half. Serve it with lemon sauce. Fine.

ROLEY POLEY PUDDING. (Apple.)

Peel, core and slice sour apples; make a rich biscuit dough, or raised biscuit dough may be used if rolled thinner; roll not quite half an inch thick, lay the slices on the paste, roll up, tuck in the ends, prick deeply with a fork, lay it in a steamer and steam hard for an hour and three-quarters. Or wrap it in a pudding-cloth well floured, tie the ends, baste up the sides, plunge into boiling water and boil continually an hour and a half, perhaps more. Stoned cherries, dried fruits, or any kind of berries, fresh or dried, may be used.

FRUIT PUFF PUDDING.

Into one pint of flour stir two teaspoonfuls baking powder and a little salt; then sift and stir the mixture into milk, until very soft. Place well-greased cups in a steamer, put in each a spoonful of the above batter, then add one of berries or steamed apples, cover with another spoonful of batter and steam twenty minutes. This pudding is delicious made with strawberries and eaten with a sauce made of two eggs, half a cup butter, a cup of sugar beaten thoroughly with a cup of boiling milk and one cup of strawberries.

SPONGE CAKE PUDDING. No. 1.

Bake a common sponge cake in a flat-bottomed pudding-dish; when ready to use, cut in six or eight pieces, split and spread with butter and return them to the dish. Make a custard with four eggs to a quart of milk; flavor and sweeten to taste; pour over the cake and bake one-half hour. The cake will swell and fill the custard. Serve with or without sauce.

SPONGE CAKE PUDDING. No. 2.

Butter pudding-mold; fill the mold with small sponge cakes or slices of stale plain cake that have been soaked in a liquid made by dissolving one-half pint of jelly in a pint of hot water. This will be of as fine a flavor and much better for all than if the cake had been soaked in wine. Make a sufficient quantity of custard to fill the mold and leave as much more to be boiled in a dish by itself. Set the mold, after being tightly covered, into a kettle and boil one hour. Turn out of the mold and serve with some of the other custard poured over it.

GRAHAM PUDDING.

Mix well together one-half a coffeecupful of molasses, one-quarter of a cupful of butter, one egg, one-half a cupful of milk, one-half a teaspoonful of pure soda, one and one-half cupfuls of good Graham flour, one small teacupful of raisins, spices to taste. Steam four hours and serve with brandy or wine sauce, or any sauce that may be preferred. This makes a showy as well as a light and wholesome dessert, and has the merit of simplicity and cheapness.

BANANA PUDDING.

Cut sponge cake in-slices, and, in a glass dish, put alternately a layer of cake and a layer of bananas sliced. Make a soft custard, flavor with a little wine, and pour over it. Beat the whites of the eggs to a stiff froth and heap over the whole.

Peaches cut up, left a few hours in sugar and then scalded, and added when cold to thick boiled custard, made rather sweet, are a delicious dessert.

DRIED PEACH PUDDING.

Boil one pint of milk and while hot turn it over a pint of bread-crumbs. Stir into it a tablespoonful of butter, one pint of dried peaches stewed soft. When all is cool, add two well-beaten eggs, half a cupful of sugar and a pinch of salt; flavor to taste. Put into a well-buttered pudding-dish and bake half an hour.

SUET PUDDING, PLAIN.

One cupful of chopped suet, one cupful of milk, two eggs beaten, half a teaspoonful of salt and enough flour to make a stiff batter, but thin enough to pour from a spoon. Put into a bowl, cover with a cloth and boil three hours. The same, made a little thinner, with a few raisins added and baked in a well-greased dish is excellent. Two teaspoonfuls of baking powder in the flour improves this pudding. Or if made with sour milk and soda it is equally as good.

SUET PLUM PUDDING.

One cupful of suet chopped fine, one cupful of cooking molasses, one cupful of milk, one cupful of raisins, three and one-half cupfuls of flour, one egg, one teaspoonful of cloves, two of cinnamon and one of nutmeg, a little salt, one teaspoonful of soda; boil three hours in a pudding-mold set into a kettle of water; eat with common sweet sauce. If sour milk is used in place of sweet, the pudding will be much lighter.

PEACH COBBLER.

Line a deep dish with rich thick crust; pare and cut into halves or quarters some juicy, rather tart peaches; put in sugar, spices and flavoring to taste; stew it slightly and put it in the lined dish; cover with thick crust of rich puff paste and bake a rich brown; when done, break up the top crust into small pieces and stir it into the fruit; serve hot or cold; very palatable without sauce, but more so with plain rich cream or cream sauce, or with a rich brandy or wine. Other fruits can be used in place of peaches. Currants are best made in this manner:—

Press the currants through a sieve to free it from pips; to each pint of the pulp put two ounces of crumbed bread and four ounces of sugar; bake with a rim of puff paste; serve with cream. White currants may be used instead of red.

HOMINY PUDDING.

Two-thirds of a cupful of hominy, one and a half pints of milk, two eggs, one tablespoonful of butter, one teaspoonful of extract of lemon or vanilla, one cupful of sugar. Boil hominy in milk one hour; then pour it on the eggs, extract and sugar beaten together; add butter, pour in buttered pudding-dish, bake in hot oven for twenty minutes.

BAKED BERRY ROLLS.

Roll rich biscuit dough thin, cut it into little squares four inches wide and seven inches long. Spread over with berries. Roll up the crust, and put the rolls in a dripping-pan just a little apart; put a piece of butter on each roll, spices if you like. Strew over a large handful of sugar, a little hot water. Set in the oven and bake like dumplings. Served with sweet sauce.

GREEN CORN PUDDING.

Take two dozen full ears of sweet green corn, score the kernels and cut them from the cob. Scrape off what remains on the cob with a knife. Add a pint and a half or one quart of milk, according to the youngness and juiciness of the corn. Add four eggs well beaten, a half teacupful of flour, a half teacupful butter, a tablespoonful of sugar, and salt to taste. Bake in a well-greased earthen dish, in hot oven two hours. Place it on the table browned and smoking hot, eat it with plenty of fresh butter. This can be used as a dessert by serving a sweet sauce with it. If eaten plainly with butter, it answers as a side vegetable.

GENEVA WAFERS.

Two eggs, three ounces of butter, three ounces of flour, three ounces of pounded sugar. Well whisk the eggs, put them into a basin and stir to them the butter, which should be beaten to a cream; add the flour and sifted sugar gradually, and then mix all well together. Butter a baking sheet, and drop on it a teaspoonful of the mixture at a time, leaving a space between each. Bake in a cool oven; watch the pieces of paste, and, when half done, roll them up like wafers and put in a small wedge of bread or piece of wood, to keep them in shape. Return them to the oven until crisp. Before serving, remove the bread, put a spoonful of preserve in the widest end, and fill up with whipped cream. This is a very pretty and ornamental dish for the supper-table, and is very nice and very easily made.

STIRRING THE CRANBERRY SAUCE.

MINUTE PUDDING. No. 1.

Set saucepan or deep frying pan on the stove, the bottom and sides well buttered, put into it a quart of sweet milk, a pinch of salt and a piece of butter as large as half an egg; when it boils have ready a dish of sifted flour, stir it into the boiling milk, sifting it through your fingers, a handful at a time, until it becomes smooth and quite thick. Turn it into a dish that has been dipped in water. Make a sauce very sweet to serve with it. Maple molasses is *fine* with it. This pudding is much improved by adding canned berries or fresh ones just before taking from the stove.

MINUTE PUDDING. No. 2.

One quart of milk, salt, two eggs, about a pint of flour. Beat the eggs well; add the flour and enough milk to make it smooth. Butter the saucepan and put in the remainder of the milk well salted; when it boils, stir in the flour, eggs, etc., lightly; let it cook well. It should be of the consistency of thick corn mush. Serve immediately with the following simple sauce, *viz*: Rich milk or cream sweetened to taste and flavored with grated nutmeg.

SUNDERLAND PUDDING.

One cupful of sugar, half a cupful of cold butter, a pint of milk, two cupfuls of sifted flour and five eggs. Make the milk hot; stir in the butter and let it cool before the other ingredients are added to it; then stir in the sugar, flour and eggs, which should be well whisked and omit the whites of two; flavor with a little grated lemon rind and beat the mixture well. Butter some small cups, rather more than half fill them; bake from twenty minutes to half an hour, according to the size of the puddings, and serve with fruit, custard or wine sauce, a little of which may be poured over them. They may be dropped by spoonfuls on buttered tins and baked, if cups are not convenient.

JELLY PUDDINGS.

Two cupfuls of *very* fine stale biscuit or bread crumbs, one cupful of rich milk—half cream, if you can get it; five eggs beaten very light, half a teaspoonful of soda stirred in boiling water, one cupful of sweet jelly, jam or marmalade. Scald the milk and pour over the crumbs. Beat until half cold and stir in the beaten yolks, then whites, finally the soda. Fill large cups half full with the batter, set in a quick oven and bake half an hour. When done, turn out quickly and dexterously; with a sharp knife make an incision in the side of each; pull partly open, and put a liberal spoonful of the conserve within. Close the slit by pinching the edges with your fingers. Eat warm with sweetened cream.

QUICK PUDDING.

Soak and split some crackers; lay the surface over with raisins and citron; put the halves together, tie them in a bag, and boil fifteen minutes in milk and water; delicious with rich sauce.

READY PUDDING.

Make a batter of one quart of milk and about one pound of flour; add six eggs, the yolks and whites separately beaten, a teaspoonful of salt and four tablespoonfuls of sugar. It should be as stiff as can possibly be stirred with a spoon. Dip a spoonful at a time into quick boiling water, boil from five to ten minutes, take out. Serve hot with sauce or syrup.

A ROYAL DESSERT.

Cut a stale cake into slices an inch and a half in thickness; pour over them a little good sweet cream; then fry *lightly* in fresh butter in a smooth frying pan; when done, place over each slice of cake a layer of preserves or you may make a rich sauce to be served with it.

Another dish equally as good, is to dip thin slices of bread into fresh milk; have ready two eggs well beaten; dip the slices in the egg and fry them in butter to a light brown; when fried, pour over them a syrup, any kind that you choose, and serve hot.

HUCKLEBERRIES WITH CRACKERS AND CREAM.

Pick over carefully one quart of blueberries and keep them on ice until wanted. Put into each bowl, for each guest, two soda crackers, broken in not too small pieces; add a few tablespoonfuls of berries, a teaspoonful of powdered sugar and fill the bowl with the richest of cold sweet cream. This is an old-fashioned New England breakfast dish. It also answers for a dessert.

SAUCES FOR PUDDINGS.

BRANDY SAUCE, COLD.

Two cupfuls of powdered sugar, half a cupful of butter, one wine-glassful of brandy, cinnamon and nutmeg, a teaspoonful of each. Warm the butter slightly and work it to a light cream with the sugar, then add the brandy and spices; beat it hard and set aside until wanted. Should be put into a mold to look nicely and serve on a flat dish.

BRANDY OR WINE SAUCE. No. 1.

Stir a heaping teaspoonful of cornstarch in a little cold water to a smooth paste (or instead use a tablespoonful of sifted flour); add to it a cupful of boiling water, with one cupful of sugar, a piece of butter as large as an egg, boil all together ten minutes. Remove from the fire and when cool stir into it half of a cupful of brandy or wine. It should be about as thick as thin syrup.

BRANDY OR WINE SAUCE. No. 2.

Take one cupful of butter, two of powdered sugar, the whites of two eggs, five tablespoonfuls of sherry wine or brandy and a quarter of a cupful of boiling water. Beat butter and sugar to a cream, add the whites of the eggs, one at a time, unbeaten, and then the wine or brandy. Place the bowl in hot water and stir till smooth and frothy.

RICH WINE SAUCE.

One cupful of butter, two of powdered sugar, half a cupful of wine. Beat the butter to a cream. Add the sugar gradually and when very light add the wine, which has been made hot, a little at a time, a teaspoonful of grated nutmeg. Place the bowl in a basin of hot water and stir for two minutes. The sauce should be smooth and foamy.

SAUCE FOR PLUM PUDDING. (Superior.)

Cream together a cupful of sugar and half a cupful of butter; when light and creamy, add the well-beaten yolks of four eggs. Stir into this one wine-glass of wine or one of brandy, a pinch of salt and one large cupful of hot cream or rich milk. Beat this mixture well; place it in a saucepan over the fire, stir it until it cooks sufficiently to thicken like cream. Be sure and not let it boil. Delicious.

LIQUID BRANDY SAUCE.

Brown over the fire three tablespoonfuls of sugar; add a cupful of water, six whole cloves and a piece of stick cinnamon, the yellow rind of a lemon cut very thin; let the sauce boil, strain while hot, then pour it into a sauce bowl containing the juice of the lemon and a cup of brandy. Serve warm.

GRANDMOTHERS SAUCE.

Cream together a cupful of sifted sugar and half a cupful of butter, add a teaspoonful of ground cinnamon and an egg well beaten. Boil a teacupful of milk and turn it, boiling hot, over the mixture slowly, stirring all the time; this will cook the egg smoothly. It may be served cold or hot.

SUGAR SAUCE.

One coffeecupful of granulated sugar, half of a cupful of water, a piece of butter the size of a walnut. Boil all together until it becomes the consistency of syrup. Flavor with lemon or vanilla extract. A tablespoonful of lemon juice is an improvement. Nice with cottage pudding.

LEMON SAUCE.

One cupful of sugar, half a cupful of butter, one egg beaten light, one lemon, juice and grated rind, half a cupful of boiling water; put in a tin basin and thicken over steam.

LEMON CREAM SAUCE, HOT.

Put half a pint of new milk on the fire and when it boils stir into it one teaspoonful of wheat flour, four ounces of sugar and the well-beaten yolks of three eggs; remove it from the fire and add the grated rind and the juice of one lemon; stir it well and serve hot in a sauce tureen.

ORANGE CREAM SAUCE, HOT.

This is made as LEMON CREAM SAUCE, substituting orange for lemon.

Creams for puddings, pies and fritters may be made in the same manner with any other flavoring; if flour is used in making them, it should boil in the milk three or four minutes.

COLD LEMON SAUCE.

Beat to a cream one teacupful of butter and two teacupfuls of fine white sugar; then stir in the juice and grated rind of one lemon; grate nutmeg upon the sauce and serve on a flat dish.

COLD ORANGE SAUCE.

Beat to a cream one teacupful of butter and two teacupfuls of fine white sugar; then stir in the grated rind of one orange and the juice of two; stir until all the orange juice is absorbed; grate nutmeg upon the sauce and serve on a flat dish.

COLD CREAM SAUCE.

Stir to a cream one cupful of sugar, half a cupful of butter, then add a cupful of sweet, thick cold cream, flavor to taste. Stir well and set it in a cool place.

CREAM SAUCE, WARM.

Heat a pint of cream slowly in a double boiler; when nearly boiling, set it off from the fire, put into it half a cupful of sugar, a little nutmeg or vanilla extract; stir it thoroughly and add, when cool, the whites of two well-beaten eggs. Set it on the fire in a dish containing hot water to keep it warm until needed, stirring once or more.

CARAMEL SAUCE.

Place over the fire a saucepan; when it begins to be hot, put into it four tablespoonfuls of white sugar and one tablespoonful of water. Stir it continually for three or four minutes, until all the water evaporates; then watch it carefully until it becomes a delicate brown color. Have ready a pint of cold water and cup of sugar mixed with some flavoring; turn it into the saucepan with the browned sugar and let it simmer for ten minutes; then add half a glass of brandy or a glass of wine. The wine or brandy may be omitted if preferred.

A GOOD PLAIN SAUCE.

A good sauce to go with plain fruit puddings is made by mixing one cupful of brown sugar, one cupful of best molasses, half a cupful of butter, one large teaspoonful of flour; add the juice and grated rind of one lemon, half a nutmeg grated, half a teaspoonful of cloves and cinnamon. When these are all stirred together, add a teacupful of boiling water; stir it constantly, put into a saucepan and let it boil until clear; then strain.

OLD STYLE SAUCE.

One pint of sour cream, the juice and finely grated rind of a large lemon; sugar to taste. Beat hard and long until the sauce is very light. This is delicious with cold "Brown Betty"—a form of cold farina—cornstarch, blanc mange and the like.

PLAIN COLD, HARD SAUCE.

Stir together one cupful of white sugar and half a cupful of butter until it is creamy and light; add flavoring to taste. This is very nice, flavored with the juice of raspberries or strawberries, or beat into it a cupful of ripe strawberries or raspberries and the white of an egg beaten stiff.

CUSTARD SAUCE.

One cupful of sugar, two beaten eggs, one pint of milk, flavoring to taste, brandy or wine, if preferred.

Heat the milk to boiling; add by degrees the beaten eggs and sugar, put in the flavoring and set within a pan of boiling water; stir until it begins to thicken; then take it off and stir in the brandy or wine gradually; set, until wanted, within a pan of boiling water.

MILK SAUCE.

Dissolve a tablespoonful of flour in cold milk; see that it is free from lumps. Whisk an ounce of butter and a cupful of sugar to a cream and add to it a pinch of salt. Mix together half a pint of milk, one egg and the flour; stir this into the butter and add a dash of nutmeg, or any flavor; heat until near the boiling point and serve. Very nice in place of cold cream.

MILK OR CREAM SAUCE.

Cream or rich milk, simply sweetened with plenty of white sugar and flavored, answers the purpose for some kinds of pudding, and can be made very quickly.

FRUIT SAUCE.

Two-thirds of a cupful of sugar, a pint of raspberries or strawberries, a tablespoonful of melted butter and a cupful of hot water. Boil all together slowly, removing the scum as fast as it rises; then strain through a sieve. This is very good served with dumplings or apple puddings.

JELLY SAUCE.

Melt two tablespoonfuls of sugar and half a cupful of jelly over the fire in a cupful of boiling water, adding also two tablespoonfuls of butter; then stir into it a teaspoonful of cornstarch, dissolved in half a cupful of water or wine; add it to the jelly and let it come to a boil. Set it in a dish of hot water to keep it warm until time to serve; stir occasionally. Any fruit jelly can be used.

COMMON SWEET SAUCE.

Into a pint of water stir a paste made of a tablespoonful of cornstarch or flour (rubbed smooth with a little cold water); add a cupful of sugar and a tablespoonful of vinegar. Cook well for three minutes. Take from the fire and add a piece of butter as large as a small egg; when cool, flavor with a tablespoonful of vanilla or lemon extract.

SYRUP FOR FRUIT SAUCE.

An excellent syrup for fruit sauce is made of Morello cherries (red, sour cherries). For each pound of cherry juice, allow half a pound of sugar and six cherry kernels; seed the cherries and let them stand in a bowl over night; in the morning, press them through a fine cloth, which has been dipped in boiling water, weigh the juice, add the sugar, boil fifteen minutes, removing all the scum. Fill small bottles that are perfectly dry with the syrup; when it is cold, cork the bottles tightly, seal them and keep them in a cool place, standing upright.

Most excellent to put into pudding sauces.

ROSE BRANDY. (For Cakes and Puddings.)

Gather the leaves of roses while the dew is on them, and as soon as they open put them into a wide-mouthed bottle, and when the bottle is full pour in the best of fourth proof French brandy.

It will be fit for use in three or four weeks and may be frequently replenished. It is sometimes considered preferable to wine as a flavoring to pastries and pudding sauces.

LEMON BRANDY. (For Cakes and Puddings.)

When you use lemons for punch or lemonade, do not throw away the peels but cut them in small pieces—the thin yellow outside (the thick part is not good)—and put them in a glass jar or bottle of brandy. You will find this brandy useful for many purposes.

In the same way keep for use the kernels of peach and plum stones, pounding them slightly before you put them into the brandy.

PRESERVES, JELLIES, ETC.

Fruit for preserving should be sound and free from all defects, using white sugar, and also that which is dry, which produces the nicest syrup; dark sugar can be used by being clarified, which is done by dissolving two pounds of sugar in a pint of water; add to it the white of an egg and beat it well, put it into a preserving kettle on the fire and stir with a wooden spoon. As soon as it begins to swell and boil up, throw in a little cold water; let it boil up again, take it off and remove the scum; boil it again, throw in more cold water and remove the scum; repeat until it is clear and pours like oil from the spoon.

In the old way of preserving, we used pound for pound, when they were kept in stone jars or crocks; now, as most preserves are put up in sealed jars or cans, less sugar seems sufficient; three-quarters of a pound of sugar is generally all that is required for a pound of fruit.

Fruit should be boiled in a porcelain-lined or granite-ware dish, if possible; but other utensils, copper or metal, if made bright and clean, answer as well.

Any of the fruits that have been preserved in syrup may be converted into dry preserves, by first draining them from the syrup, and then drying them in a stove or very moderate oven, adding to them a quantity of powdered loaf sugar, which will gradually penetrate the fruit, while the fluid parts of the syrup gently evaporate. They should be dried in the stove or oven on a sieve, and turned every six or eight hours, fresh powdered sugar being sifted over them every time they are turned. Afterwards they are to be kept in a dry situation, in drawers or boxes. Currants and cherries preserved whole in this manner, in bunches, are extremely elegant and have a fine flavor. In this way it is, also, that orange and lemon chips are preserved.

Mold can be prevented from forming on fruit jellies by pouring a little melted paraffine over the top. When cool, it will harden to a solid cake, winch can be easily removed when the jelly is used, and saved to use over again another year. It is perfectly harmless and tasteless.

Large glass tumblers are the best for keeping jellies, much better than large vessels, for by being opened frequently they soon spoil; a paper should be cut to fit and placed over the jelly; then put on the lid or cover, with thick paper rubbed over on the inside with the white of an egg.

There cannot be too much care taken in selecting fruit for jellies, for if the fruit is over ripe, any amount of time in boiling will never make it jelly—there is where so many fail in making good jelly; and another important matter is overlooked—that of carefully skimming off the juice after it begins to boil and a scum rises from the bottom to the top; the juice should not be stirred, but the scum carefully taken off; if allowed to boil under, the jelly will not be clear.

When either preserves or canned fruits show any indications of fermentation, they should be immediately re-boiled with more sugar, to save them. It is much better to be generous with the sugar at first than to have any losses afterwards. Keep all preserves in a cool, dry closet.

PRESERVED CHERRIES.

Take large, ripe Morello cherries; weigh them and to each pound allow a pound of loaf sugar. Stone the cherries (opening them with a sharp quill) and save the juice that comes from them in the process. As you stone them, throw them into a large pan or tureen and strew about half the sugar over them and let them lie in it an hour or two after they are all stoned. Then put them into a preserving kettle with the remainder of the sugar and boil and skim them till the fruit is clear and the syrup thick.

PRESERVED CRANBERRIES.

The cranberries must be large and ripe. Wash them and to six quarts of cranberries allow nine pounds of the beat loaf sugar. Take three quarts of the cranberries and put them into a stewpan with a pint and a half of water.

Cover the pan and boil or stew them till they are all to pieces. Then squeeze the juice through a jelly bag. Put the sugar into a preserving kettle, pour the cranberry juice over it and let it stand until it is all melted, stirring it up frequently. Then place the kettle over the fire and put in the remaining three quarts of whole cranberries. Let them boil till they are tender, clear and of a bright color, skimming them frequently. When done, put them warm into jars with the syrup, which should be like a thick jelly.

PRESERVED STRAWBERRIES.

For every pound of fruit weigh a pound of refined sugar; put them with the sugar over the fire in a porcelain kettle, bring to a boil slowly about twenty minutes. Take them out carefully with a perforated skimmer and fill your *hot* jars nearly full; boil the juice a few minutes longer and fill up the jars; seal them *hot*. Keep in a cool, dry place.

TO PRESERVE BERRIES WHOLE. (Excellent.)

Buy the fruit when not *too ripe*, pick over immediately, wash if absolutely necessary and put in glass jars, filling each one about two-thirds full.

Put in the preserving kettle a pound of sugar and one cupful of water for every two pounds of fruit, and let it come slowly to a boil. Pour this syrup into the jars over the berries, filling them up to the brim; then set the jars in a pot of *cold* water on the stove, and let the water boil and the fruit become scalding hot. Now take them out and seal perfectly tight. If this process is followed thoroughly, the fruit will keep for several years.

PRESERVED EGG PLUMS.

Use a pound of sugar for a pound of plums; wash the plums and wipe dry; put the sugar on a slow fire in the preserving kettle, with as much water as will melt the sugar and let it simmer slowly; then prick each plum thoroughly with a needle, or a fork with fine prongs, and place a layer of them in the syrup; let them cook until they lose their color a little and the skins begin to break; then lift them out with a perforated skimmer and place them singly in a large dish to cool; then put another layer of plums in the syrup and let them cook and cool in the same manner, until the whole are done; as they cool, carefully replace the broken skins so as not to spoil the appearance of the plums; when the last layer is finished, return the first to the kettle, and boil until transparent; do the same with each layer; while the latest cooked are cooling, place the first in glass jars; when all are done, pour the hot syrup over them; when they are cold, close as usual; the jelly should be of the color and consistency of rich wine jelly.

PRESERVED PEACHES.

Peaches for preserving may be ripe but not soft; cut them in halves, take out the stones and pare them neatly; take as many pounds of white sugar as of fruit, put to each pound of sugar a teacupful of water; stir it until it is dissolved; set it over a moderate fire; when it is boiling hot, put in the peaches; let them boil gently until a pure, clear, uniform color; turn those at the bottom to the top carefully with a skimmer several times; do not hurry them. When they are clear, take each half up with a spoon and spread them on flat dishes to become cold. When all are done, let the syrup boil until it is quite thick; pour it into a large pitcher and let it set to cool and settle. When the peaches are cold put them carefully into jars and pour the syrup over them, leaving any sediment which has settled at the bottom, or strain the syrup. Some of the kernels from the peach-stones may be put in with the peaches while boiling. Let them remain open one night, then cover.

In like manner quince, plum, apricot, apple, cherry, greengage and other fruit preserves are made; in every case fine large fruit should be taken, free from imperfections, and the slightest bruises or other fault should be removed.

PRESERVED GREEN TOMATOES.

Take one peck of green tomatoes. Slice six fresh lemons without removing the skins, but taking out the seeds; put to this quantity six pounds of sugar, common white, and boil until transparent and the syrup thick. Ginger root may be added, if liked.

PRESERVED APPLES. (Whole.)

Peel and core large firm apples (pippins are best). Throw them into water as you pare them. Boil the parings in water for fifteen minutes, allowing a pint to one pound of fruit. Then strain and, adding three-quarters of a pound of sugar to each pint of water, as measured at first, with enough lemon peel, orange peel or mace, to impart a pleasant flavor, return to the kettle. When the syrup has been well skimmed and is clear, pour it boiling hot over the apples, which must be drained from the water in which they have hitherto stood. Let them remain in the syrup until both are perfectly cold. Then, covering closely, let them simmer over a slow fire until transparent. When all the minutiæ of these directions are attended to, the fruit will remain unbroken and present a beautiful and inviting appearance.

PRESERVED QUINCES.

Pare, core and quarter your fruit, then weigh it and allow an equal quantity of white sugar. Take the parings and cores and put in a preserving kettle; cover them with water and boil for half an hour; then strain through a hair-sieve, and put the juice back into the kettle and boil the quinces in it a little at a time until they are tender; lift out as they are done with a drainer and lay on a dish; if the liquid seems scarce add more water. When all are cooked, throw into this liquor the sugar, and allow it to boil ten minutes before putting in the quinces; let them boil until they change color, say one hour and a quarter, on a slow fire; while they are boiling occasionally slip a silver spoon under them to see that they do not burn, but on no account stir them. Have two fresh lemons cut in thin slices, and when the fruit is being put in jars lay a slice or two in each. Quinces may be steamed until tender.

PRESERVED PEARS.

One pound of fruit, one pound of sugar; pare off the peeling thin. Make a nice syrup of nearly one cupful of water and one pound of sugar, and when clarified by boiling and skimming put in the pears and stew gently until clear. Choose rather pears like the Seckle for preserving, both on account of the flavor and size. A nice way is to stick a clove in the blossom end of each pear, for this fruit seems to require some extraneous flavor to bring out its own piquancy. Another acceptable addition to pear preserves may be found instead, by adding the juice and thinly pared rind of one lemon to each five pounds of fruit. If the pears are hard and tough, parboil them until tender before beginning to preserve, and from the same water take what you need for making their syrup.

If you can procure only large pears to preserve, cut them into halves, or even slices, so that they can get done more quickly, and lose nothing in appearance, either.

PINEAPPLE PRESERVES.

Twist off the top and bottom and pare off the rough outside of pineapples; then weigh them and cut them in slices, chips or quarters, or cut them in four or six and shape each piece like a whole pineapple; to each pound of fruit, put a teacupful of water; put it in a preserving kettle, cover it and set it over the fire and let them boil gently until they are tender and clear; then take them from the water, by sticking a fork in the centre of each slice, or with a skimmer, into a dish.

Put to the water white sugar, a pound for each pound of fruit; stir it until it is all dissolved; then put in the pineapple, cover the kettle and boil them gently until transparent throughout; when it is so, take it out, let it cool and put it in glass jars; let the syrup boil or simmer gently until it is thick and rich and when nearly cool, pour it over the fruit. The next day secure the jars, as before directed.

Pineapple done in this way is a beautiful and delicious preserve. The usual manner of preserving it by putting it into the syrup without first boiling it, makes it little better than sweetened leather.

TO PRESERVE WATERMELON RIND AND CITRON.

Pare off the green skin, cut the watermelon rind into pieces. Weigh the pieces and allow to each pound a pound and a half of loaf sugar. Line your kettle with green vine-leaves, and put in the pieces *without* the sugar. A layer of vine-leaves must cover each layer of melon rind. Pour in water to cover the whole and place a thick cloth over the kettle. Simmer the fruit for two hours, after scattering a few bits of alum amongst it. Spread the melon rind on a dish to cool. Melt the sugar, using a pint of water to a pound and a half of sugar, and mix with it some beaten white of egg. Boil and skim the sugar. When quite clear, put in the rind and let it boil two hours; take out the rind, boil the syrup again, pour it over the rind, and let it remain all night. The next morning, boil the syrup with lemon juice, allowing one lemon to a quart of syrup. When it is thick enough to hang in a drop from the point of a spoon, it is done. Put the rind in jars and pour over it the syrup. It is not fit for use immediately.

Citrons may be preserved in the same manner, first paring off the outer skin and cutting them into quarters. Also green limes.

TO PRESERVE AND DRY GREENGAGES.

To every pound of sugar allow one pound of fruit, one quarter pint of water.

For this purpose, the fruit must be used before it is quite ripe and part of the stalk must be left on. Weigh the fruit, rejecting all that is in the least degree blemished, and put it into a lined saucepan with the sugar and water, which should have been previously boiled together to a rich syrup. Boil the fruit in this for ten minutes, remove it from the fire, and drain the greengages. The next day boil up the syrup and put in the fruit again, let it simmer for three minutes, and drain the syrup away. Continue this process for five or six days, and the last time place the greengages, when drained, on a hair-sieve, and put them in an oven or warm spot to dry; keep them in a box, with paper between each layer, in a place free from damp.

PRESERVED PUMPKINS.

To each pound of pumpkin allow one pound of roughly pounded loaf sugar, one gill of lemon juice.

Obtain a good, sweet pumpkin; halve it, take out the seeds and pare off the rind; cut it into neat slices. Weigh the pumpkin, put the slices in a pan or deep dish in layers, with the sugar sprinkled between them; pour the lemon juice over the top, and let the whole remain for two or three days. Boil all together, adding half a pint of water to every three pounds of sugar used until the pumpkin becomes tender; then turn the whole into a pan, where let it remain for a week; then drain off the syrup, boil it until it is quite thick, skim, and pour it boiling over the pumpkin. A little bruised ginger and lemon rind, thinly pared, may be boiled in the syrup to flavor the pumpkin.

A Southern Recipe.

PRESERVING FRUIT. (New Mode.)

Housekeepers who dislike the tedious, old-time fashion of clarifying sugar and boiling the fruit, will appreciate, the following two recipes, no fire being needed in their preparation. The first is for "tutti frutti," and has been repeatedly tested with unvarying success.

Put one quart of white, preserving, fine Batavia brandy into a two-gallon stone jar that has a tightly fitting top. Then for every pound of fruit, in prime condition and perfectly dry, which you put in the brandy, use three-quarters of a pound of granulated sugar; stir every day so that the sugar will be dissolved, using a clean, wooden spoon kept for the purpose. Every sort of fruit may be used, beginning with strawberries and ending with plums. Be sure and have at least one pound of black cherries, as they make the color of the preserve very rich. Strawberries, raspberries, blackberries, apricots, cherries (sweet and sour), peaches, plums, are all used, and, if you like, currants and grapes. Plums and grapes should be peeled and seeded, apricots and peaches peeled and cut in quarters or eighths or dice; cherries also must be seeded; quinces may be steamed until tender. The jar must be kept in a cool, dry place, and the daily stirring must never be forgotten, for that is the secret of success. You may use as much of one sort of fruit as you like, and it may be put in from day to day, just as you happen to have it. Half the quantity of spirits may be used. The preserve will be ready for use within a week after the last fruit is put in, and will keep for a number of months. We have found it good eight months after making.

The second is as follows: Take some pure white vinegar and mix with it granulated sugar until a syrup is formed quite free from acidity. Pour this syrup into earthen jars and put in it good, perfectly ripe fruit, gathered in dry weather. Cover the jars tight and put them in a dry place. The contents will keep for six or eight months, and the flavor of the fruit will be excellent.

TO PRESERVE FRUIT WITHOUT 'SUGAR.

Cherries, strawberries, sliced pineapple, plums, apricots, gooseberries, etc., may be preserved in the following manner—to be used the same as fresh fruit.

Gather the fruit before it is very ripe; put it in wide-mouthed bottles made for the purpose; fill them as full as they will hold and cork them tight; seal the corks; put some hay in a large saucepan, set in the bottles, with hay between them to prevent their touching; then fill the saucepan with water to the necks of the bottles, and set it over the fire until the water is nearly boiled, then take it off; let it stand until the bottles are cold. Keep them in a cool place until wanted, when the fruit will be found equal to fresh.

NEW METHOD OF PRESERVING FRUIT.

A new method of preserving fruit is practiced in England. Pears, apples and other fruits are reduced to a paste by jamming, which is then pressed into cakes and gently dried. When required for use it is only necessary to pour four times their weight of boiling water over them and allow them to soak for twenty minutes and then add sugar to suit the taste. The fine flavor of the fruit is said to be retained to perfection. The cost of the prepared product is scarcely greater than that of the original fruit, differing with the supply and price of the latter; the keeping qualities are excellent, so that it may be had at any time of the year and bears long sea-voyages with out detriment. No peeling or coring is required, so there is no waste.

FRUIT JELLIES.

Take a stone jar and put in the fruit, place this in a kettle of tepid water and set on the fire; let it boil, closely covered, until the fruit is broken to pieces; strain, pressing the bag, a stout, coarse one, hard, putting in a few handfuls each time, and between each squeezing turning it inside out to scald off the pulp and skins; to each pint of juice allow a pound of loaf sugar; set the juice on alone to boil, and, while it is boiling, put the sugar into shallow dishes or pans, and heat it in the oven, watching and stirring it to prevent burning; boil the juice just twenty minutes from the time it begins fairly to boil; by this time the sugar should be *very* hot; throw it into the boiling juice, stirring rapidly all the time; withdraw the spoon when all is thoroughly dissolved; let the jelly come to a boil to make all certain; withdraw the kettle instantly from the fire; roll your glasses and cups in hot water, and fill with the scalding liquid; the jelly will form within an hour; when cold, close and tie up as you do preserves.

CURRANT JELLY.

Currants for jelly should be perfectly ripe and gathered the *first* week of the season; they lose their jelly property if they hang on the bushes too long, and become too juicy—the juice will not be apt to congeal. Strip them from the stalks, put them into a stone jar, and set in a vessel of hot water over the fire; keep the water around it boiling until the currants are all broken, stirring them up occasionally. Then squeeze them through a coarse cloth or towel. To each pint of juice allow a pound and a quarter of refined sugar. Put the sugar into a porcelain kettle, pour the juice over it, stirring frequently. Skim it before it boils; boil about twenty minutes, or until it congeals in the spoon when held in the air. Pour it into hot jelly glasses and seal when cool.

Wild frost grape jelly is nice made after this recipe.

CURRANT JELLY. (New Method.)

This recipe for making superior jelly without heat is given in a Parisian journal of chemistry, which may be worth trying by some of our readers. The currants are to be washed and squeezed in the usual way, and the juice placed in a stone or earthen vessel, and set away in a cool place in the cellar. In about twenty-four hours a considerable amount of froth will cover the surface, produced by fermentation, and this must be removed and the whole strained again through the jelly bag, then weighed, and an equal weight of powdered white sugar is to be added. This is to be stirred constantly until entirely dissolved, and then put into jars, tied up tightly and set away. At the end of another twenty-four hours a perfectly transparent jelly of the most satisfactory flavor will be formed, which will keep as long as if it had been cooked.

QUINCE JELLY.

Quinces for jelly should not be quite ripe, they should be a fine yellow; rub off the down from them, core and cut them small; put them in a preserving kettle with a teacupful of water for each pound; let them stew gently until soft, without mashing; put them in a thin muslin bag with the liquor; press them very lightly; to each pint of the liquor put a pound of sugar; stir it until it is all dissolved, then set it over the fire and let it boil gently, until by cooling some on a plate you find it a good jelly; then turn it into pots or tumblers and, when cold, secure as directed for jellies.

RASPBERRY JELLY.

To each pint of juice allow one pound of sugar. Let the raspberries be freshly gathered, quite ripe, pick from the stalks; put them into a large jar after breaking the fruit a little with a wooden spoon, and place this jar, covered, in a saucepan of boiling water. When the juice is well drawn, which will be in from three-quarters to one hour, strain the fruit through a fine hair-sieve or cloth; measure the juice, and to every pint allow the above proportion of white sugar. Put the juice and sugar into a preserving pan, place it over the fire, and boil gently until the jelly thickens, when a little is poured on a plate; carefully remove all the scum as it rises, pour the jelly into small pots, cover down, and keep in a dry place. This jelly answers for making raspberry cream and for flavoring various sweet dishes, when, in winter, the fresh fruit is not obtainable.

APPLE JELLY.

Select apples that are rather tart and highly flavored; slice them without paring; place in a porcelain preserving kettle, cover with water, and let them cook slowly until the apples look red. Pour into a colander, drain off the juice, and let this run through a jelly-bag; return to the kettle, which must be carefully washed, and boil half an hour; measure it and allow to every pint of juice a pound of sugar and half the juice of a lemon; boil quickly for ten minutes.

The juice of apples boiled in shallow vessels, without a particle of sugar, makes the most sparkling, delicious jelly imaginable. Red apples will give jelly the color and clearness of claret, while that from light fruit is like amber. Take the cider just as it is made, not allowing it to ferment at all, and, if possible, boil it in a pan, flat, very large and shallow.

GRAPE JELLY.

Mash well the berries so as to remove the skins; pour all into a preserving kettle and cook slowly for a few minutes to extract the juice; strain through a colander, and then through a flannel jelly-bag, keeping as hot as possible, for if not allowed to cool before putting again on the stove the jelly conies much stiffer; a few quince seeds boiled with the berries the first time tend to stiffen it; measure the juice, allowing a pound of sugar to every pint of juice, and boil fast for at least half an hour. Try a little, and if it seems done, remove and put into glasses.

FLORIDA ORANGE JELLY.

Grate the yellow rind of two Florida oranges and two lemons, and squeeze the juice into a porcelain-lined preserving kettle, adding the juice of two more oranges, and removing all the seeds; put in the grated rind a quarter of a pound of sugar, or more if the fruit is sour, and a gill of water, and boil these ingredients together until a rich syrup is formed; meantime, dissolve two ounces of gelatine in a quart of warm water, stirring it over the fire until it is entirely dissolved, then add the syrup, strain the jelly, and cool it in molds wet in cold water.

CRAB-APPLE JELLY.

The apples should be juicy and ripe. The fruit is then quartered, the black spots in the cores removed, afterward put into a preserving kettle over the fire, with a teacupful of water in the bottom to prevent burning; more water is added as it evaporates while cooking. When boiled to a pulp, strain the apples through a coarse flannel, then proceed as for currant jelly.

PEACH JELLY.

Pare the peaches, take out the stones, then slice them; add to them about a quarter of the kernels. Place them in a kettle with enough water to cover them. Stir them often until the fruit is well cooked, then strain, and to every pint of the juice add the juice of a lemon; measure again, allowing a pound of sugar to each pint of juice; heat the sugar very hot, and add when the juice has boiled twenty minutes; let it come to a boil and take instantly from the fire.

ORANGE SYRUP.

Pare the oranges, squeeze and strain the juice from the pulp. To one pint of juice allow one pound and three-quarters of loaf sugar. Put the juice and sugar together, boil and skim it until it is cream; then strain it through a flannel bag and let it stand until it becomes cool, then put in bottles and cork tight.

Lemon syrup is made in the same way, except that you scald the lemons and squeeze out the juice, allowing rather more sugar.

ORANGE MARMALADE.

Allow pound for pound. Pare half the oranges and cut the rind into shreds. Boil in three waters until tender and set aside. Grate the rind of the remaining oranges; take off, and throw away every bit of the thick white inner skin; quarter all the oranges and take out the seeds. Chop or cut them into small pieces; drain all the juice that will come away without pressing them over the sugar; heat this, stirring until the sugar is dissolved, adding a *very* little water, unless the oranges are very juicy. Boil and skim five or six minutes; put in the boiled shreds and cook ten minutes; then the chopped fruit and grated peel, and boil twenty minutes longer. When cold, put into small jars, tied up with bladder or paper next the fruit, cloths dipped in wax over all. A nicer way still is to put away in tumblers with self-adjusting metal tops. Press brandied tissue paper down closely to the fruit.

LEMON MARMALADE

Is made as you would prepare orange—allowing a pound and a quarter of sugar to a pound of the fruit, and using but half the grated peel.

RAISINS. (A French Marmalade.)

This recipe is particularly valuable at seasons when fruit is scarce. Take six fine large cooking apples, peel them, put them over a slow fire, together with a wine-glass of Medeira wine and half a pound of sugar. When well stewed, split and stone two and a half pounds of raisins, and put them to stew with the apples and enough water to prevent their burning. When all appears well dissolved, beat it through a strainer bowl, and lastly through a sieve. Mold, if you like, or put away in small preserve jars, to cut in thin slices for the ornamentation of pastry, or to dish up for eating with cream.

STRAWBERRY JAM.

To each pound of fine and not too ripe berries, allow three-quarters of a pound of sugar. Put them into a preserving pan and stir gently, not to break up the fruit; simmer for one-half hour and put into pots air-tight. An excellent way to seal jellies and jams is as the German women do: cut round covers from writing paper a half-inch too large for the tops, smear the inside with the unbeaten white of an egg, tie over with a cord, and it will dry quickly and be absolutely preservative. A circular paper dipped in brandy and laid over the toothsome contents before covering, will prevent any dampness from affecting the flavor. I have removed covers heavy with mold to find the preserve intact.

GOOSEBERRY JAM.

Pick the gooseberries just as they begin to turn. Stem, wash and weigh. To four pounds of fruit add half a teacupful of water; boil until soft and add four pounds of sugar and boil until clear. If picked at the right stage the jam will be amber colored and firm, and very much nicer than if the fruit is preserved when ripe.

BRANDIED PEACHES OR PEARS.

Four pounds of fruit, four pounds of sugar, one pint of best white brandy. Make a syrup of the sugar and enough water to dissolve it. Let this come to a boil; put the fruit in and boil five minutes. Having removed the fruit carefully, let the syrup boil fifteen minutes longer, or until it thickens well; add the brandy and take the kettle at once from the fire; pour the hot syrup over the fruit and seal. If, after the fruit is taken from the fire, a reddish liquor oozes from it, drain this off before adding the clear syrup. Put up in glass jars. Peaches and pears should be peeled for brandying. Plums should be pricked and watched carefully for fear of bursting.

RASPBERRY JAM.

To five or six pounds of fine red raspberries (not too ripe) add an equal quantity of the finest quality of white sugar. Mash the whole well in a preserving kettle; add about one quart of currant juice (a little less will do) and boil gently till it jellies upon a cold plate; then put into small jars; cover with brandied paper and tie a thick white paper over them. Keep in a dark, dry and cool place.

Blackberry or strawberry jam is made the same way, leaving out the currant juice.

A NEW WAY OF KEEPING FRUIT.

It is stated that experiments have been made in keeping fruit in jars covered only with cotton batting, and at the end of two years the fruit was sound. The following directions are given for the process: Use crocks, stone butter-jars or any other convenient dishes. Prepare and cook the fruit precisely as for canning in glass jars; fill your dishes with fruit while hot and immediately cover with cotton batting, securely tied on. Remember that all putrefaction is caused by the invisible creatures in the air. Cooking the fruit expels all these, and they cannot pass through the cotton batting. The fruit thus protected will keep an indefinite period. It will be remembered that Tyndall has proved that the atmospheric germs cannot pass through a layer of cotton.

MACEDOINES.

Suspend in the centre of the jelly mold a bunch of grapes, cherries, berries, or currants on their stems, sections of oranges, pineapples, or brandied fruits, and pour in a little jelly when quite cold, but not set. It makes a very agreeable effect. By a little ingenuity you can imbed first one fruit and then another, arranging in circles, and pour a little jelly successively over each. Do not re-heat the jelly, but keep it in a warm place, while the mold is on ice and the first layers are hardening.

CANNED FRUITS

Berries and all ripe, mellow fruit require but little cooking, only long enough for the sugar to penetrate. Strew sugar over them, allow them to stand a few hours, then merely scald with the sugar; half to three-quarters of a pound is considered sufficient. Harder fruits like pears, quinces, etc., require longer boiling. The great secret of canning is to make the fruit or vegetable perfectly air-tight. It must be put up boiling hot and the vessel filled to the brim.

Have your jars conveniently placed near your boiling fruit, in a tin pan of hot water on the stove, roll them in the hot water, then fill immediately with the hot, scalding fruit, fill to the top, and seal quickly with the tops, which should also be heated; occasionally screw down the tops tighter, as the fruit shrinks as it cools, and the glass contracts and allows the air to enter the cans. They must be perfectly air-tight. The jars to be kept in a dark, cool, dry place.

Use glass jars for fruit always, and the fruit should be cooked in a porcelain or granite-iron kettle. If you are obliged to use common large-mouthed bottles with corks, steam the corks and pare them to a close fit, driving them in with a mallet. Use the following wax for sealing: One pound of resin, three ounces of beeswax, one and one-half ounces of tallow. Use a brush in covering the corks and as they cool, dip the mouth into the melted wax. Place in a basin of cold water. Pack in a cool, dark and dry cellar. After one week, examine for flaws, cracks or signs of ferment.

The rubber rings used to assist in keeping the air from the fruit cans sometimes become so dry and brittle as to be almost useless. They can be restored to normal condition usually by letting them lie in water in which you have put a little ammonia. Mix in this proportion: One part of ammonia and two parts water. Sometimes they do not need to lie in this more than five minutes, but frequently a half hour is needed to restore their elasticity.

CANNED PEACHES.

To one pound of peaches allow half a pound of sugar; to six pounds of sugar add half a tumbler of water; put in the kettle a layer of sugar and one of peaches until the whole of both are in. Wash about eight peach leaves, tie them up and put into the kettle, remembering to take them out when you begin to fill up the jars. Let the sugared fruit remain on the range, but away from the fire, until upon tipping the vessel to one side you can see some liquid; then fill the jars, taking them out of hot water into which they were put when cold, remaining until it was made to boil around them. In this way you will find out if the glass has been properly annealed; for we consider glass jars with stoppers screwing down upon India-rubber rings as the best for canning fruit in families. They should be kept in a dark closet; and although somewhat more expensive than tin in the first instance, are much nicer and keep for years with careful usage.

Fruit must be of fine flavor and *ripe*, though not *soft*, to make nice canned fruit.

Peaches should be thrown into cold water as they are peeled, to prevent a yellowish crust.

CANNED GRAPES.

There is no fruit so difficult to can nicely as the grape; by observing the following instructions you will find the grapes rich and tender a year from putting up. Squeeze the pulp from the skin, as the seeds are objectionable; boil the pulp, until the seeds begin to loosen, in one kettle, having the skins boiling, in a little water, hard in another kettle, as they are tough. When the pulp seems tender, put it through the sieve; then add the skins, if tender, with the water they boil in, if not too much. We use a large coffeecupful of sugar for a quart can; boil until thick and can in the usual way.

CANNED STRAWBERRIES.

After the berries are picked over, let as many as can be put carefully in the preserve kettle at once be placed on a platter. To each pound of fruit add three-fourths of a pound of sugar; let them stand two or three hours, till the juice is drawn from them; pour it into the kettle and let it come to a boil and remove the scum which rises; then put in the berries very carefully. As soon as they come thoroughly to a boil put them in warm jars and seal while boiling hot.

TO CAN QUINCES.

Cut the quinces into thin slices like apples for pies. To one quart jarful of quince, take a coffeesaucer and a half of sugar and a coffeecupful of water; put the sugar and water on the fire, and when boiling put in the quinces; have ready the jars with their fastenings, stand the jars in a pan of boiling water on the stove, and when the quince is clear and tender put rapidly into the jars, fruit and syrup together. The jars must be filled so that the syrup overflows, and fastened up tight as quickly as possible.

CANNED PINEAPPLE.

For six pounds of fruit, when cut and ready to can, make syrup with two and a half pounds of sugar and nearly three pints of water; boil syrup five minutes and skim or strain if necessary; then add the fruit and let it boil up; have cans hot, fill and shut up as soon as possible. Use the best white sugar. As the cans cool, keep tightening them up. Cut the fruit half an inch thick.

CANNED FRUIT JUICES.

Canned fruit juices are an excellent substitute for brandy or wine in all puddings and sauces, etc.

It is a good plan to can the pure juices of fruit in the summer time, putting it by for this purpose.

Select clean ripe fruit, press out the juice and strain it through a flannel cloth. To each pint of juice add one cupful of white granulated sugar. Put it in a porcelain kettle, bring it to the boiling point, and bottle while hot in small bottles. It must be sealed very tight while it is *hot*. Will keep a long time, the same as canned fruit.

CANNED TOMATOES.

Canning tomatoes is quite a simple process. A large or small quantity may be done at a time, and they should be put in glass jars in preference to those of tin, which are apt to injure the flavor. Very ripe tomatoes are the best for the purpose. They are first put into a large pan and covered with boiling water. This loosens the skin, which is easily removed, and the tomatoes are then put into the preserving kettle, set over a moderate fire without the addition of water or any seasoning, and brought to a boil. After boiling slowly one-half hour, they are put into the jars while boiling hot and sealed tightly. They will keep two or three years in this way. The jars should be filled to the brim to prevent air from getting in, and set in a cool, dark closet.

TO CAN CORN.

Split the kernels lengthwise with a knife, then scrape with the back of the knife, thus leaving the hulls upon the cob. Fill cans full of cut corn, pressing it in very hard. To press the corn in the can, use the small end of a potato masher, as this will enter the can easily. It will take from ten to a dozen large ears of corn to fill a one-quart can. When the cans are full, screw cover on with thumb and first finger; this will be tight enough, then place a cloth in the bottom of a wash boiler to prevent breakage. On this put a layer of cans in any position you prefer, over the cans put a layer of cloth, then a layer of cans. Fill the boiler in this manner, then cover the cans well with cold water, place the boiler on the fire and *boil* three hours without ceasing. On steady boiling depends much of your success. After boiling three hours, lift the boiler from the fire, let the water cool, then take the cans from the boiler and tighten, let them remain until cold, then tighten again. Wrap each can in brown paper to exclude the light and keep in a cool, dry cellar and be very sure the rubber rings are not hardened by use. The rings should be renewed every two years. I would advise the beginner to use new rings entirely, for poor rings cause the loss of canned fruit and vegetables in many cases. You will observe that in canning corn the cans are not wrapped in a cloth nor heated; merely filled with the cut corn. The corn in the can will shrink considerable in boiling, but on no account open them after canning.

TO CAN PEAS.

Fill the can full of peas, shake the can so they can be filled well. You cannot press the peas in the can as you did the corn, but by shaking the cans they may be filled quite full. Pour into the cans enough cold water to fill to overflowing, then screw the cover tight as you can with your thumb and first finger and proceed exactly as in canning corn.

String beans are cut as for cooking and canned in the same manner. No seasoning of salt, pepper or sugar should be added.

Mary Currier Parsons.

CANNED PLUMS.

To every pound of plums allow a quarter of a pound of sugar. Put the sugar and plums alternately into the preserving kettle, first pricking the plums to prevent their breaking. Let them stand on the back of the stove for an hour or two, then put them over a moderate fire and allow to come to a boil; skim and pour at once into jars, running a silver spoon handle around the inside of the jar to break the air-bubbles; cover and screw down the tops.

CANNED MINCE MEAT.

Mince meat for pies can be preserved for years if canned the same as fruit while *hot*, and put into glass jars and sealed perfectly tight, and set in a cool, dark place. One glass quart jar will hold enough to make two ordinary-sized pies, and in this way "mince pies" can be had in the middle of summer as well as in winter, and if the cans are sealed properly, the meat will be just as fine when opened as when first canned.

CANNED BOILED CIDER.

Boiled cider, in our grandmothers' time, was indispensable to the making of a good "mince pie," adding the proper flavor and richness, which cannot be substituted by any other ingredient, and a gill of which being added to a rule of "fruit cake" makes it more moist, keeps longer, and is far superior to fruit cake made without it. Boiled cider is an article rarely found in the market, nowadays, but can be made by any one, with but little trouble and expense, using *sweet* cider, shortly after it is made, and before fermentation takes place. Place five quarts of *sweet* cider in a porcelain-lined kettle over the fire, boil it slowly until reduced to one quart, carefully watching it that it does not burn; turn into glass jars while hot and seal tightly, the same as canned fruit. It is then ready to use any time of the year.

CANNED PUMPKIN.

Pumpkins or squash canned are far more convenient for ready use than those dried in the old-fashioned way.

Cut up pumpkin or squash into small pieces, first cutting off the peel; stew them until tender, add no seasoning; then mash them very fine with a potato masher. Have ready your cans, made hot, and then fill them with the hot pumpkin or squash, seal tight; place in a dark, cool closet.

PEACH BUTTER.

Pare ripe peaches and put them in a preserving kettle, with sufficient water to boil them soft; then sift through a colander, removing the stones. To each quart of peaches put one and one-half pounds of sugar, and boil very slowly one hour. Stir often and do not let them burn. Put in stone or glass jars, and keep in a cool place.

PEACHES DRIED WITH SUGAR.

Peel yellow peaches, cut them from the stone in one piece; allow two pounds of sugar to six pounds of fruit; make a syrup of three-quarters of a pound of sugar and a little water; put in the peaches, a few at a time, and let them cook gently until quite clear. Take them up carefully on a dish and set them in the sun to dry. Strew powdered sugar over them on all sides, a little at a time; if any syrup is left, remove to fresh dishes. When they are quite dry, lay them lightly in a jar with a little sugar sifted between the layers.

COLORING FOR FRUIT, ETC.

RED OR PINK COLORING.

Take two cents' worth of cochineal. Lay it on a flat plate and bruise it with the blade of a knife. Put it into half a teacupful of alcohol. Let it stand a quarter of an hour, and then filter it through fine muslin. Always ready for immediate use. Cork the bottle tight.

Strawberry or cranberry juice makes a fine coloring for frosting, sweet puddings and confectionery.

DEEP RED COLORING.

Take twenty grains of cochineal and fifteen grains of cream of tartar finely powdered; add to them a piece of alum the size of a cherry stone and boil them with a gill of soft water in an earthen vessel, slowly, for half an hour. Then strain it through muslin, and keep it tightly corked in a phial. If a little alcohol is added it will keep any length of time.

YELLOW COLORING.

Take a little saffron, put it into an earthen vessel with a very small quantity of cold, soft water, and let it steep till the color of the infusion is a bright yellow. Then strain it, add half alcohol to it. To color fruit yellow, boil the fruit with fresh lemon skins in water to cover them until it is tender; then take it up, spread it on dishes to cool and finish as may be directed.

To color icing, put the grated peel of a lemon or orange in a thin muslin bag, squeezing a little juice through it, then mixing with the sugar.

GREEN COLORING.

Take fresh spinach or beet leaves and pound them in a marble mortar. If you want it for immediate use, take off the green froth as it rises, and mix it with the article you intend to color. If you wish to keep it a few days, take the juice when you have pressed out a teacupful, and adding to it a piece of alum the size of a pea, give it a boil in a saucepan. Or make the juice very strong and add a quart of alcohol. Bottle it air-tight.

SUGAR GRAINS.

These are made by pounding white lump sugar in a mortar and shaking it through sieves of different degrees of coarseness, thus accumulating grains of different sizes. They are used in ornamenting cake.

SUGAR GRAINS, COLORED.

Stir a little coloring—as the essence of spinach, or prepared cochineal, or liquid carmine, or indigo, rouge, saffron, etc.,—into the sugar grains made as above, until each grain is stained, then spread them on a baking-sheet and dry them in a warm place. They are used in ornamenting cake.

CARAMEL OR BURNT SUGAR.

Put one cupful of sugar and two teaspoonfuls of water in a saucepan on the fire; stir constantly until it is quite a dark color, then add a half cupful of water and a pinch of salt; let it boil a few minutes and when cold, bottle.

For coloring soups, sauces or gravies.

TO CLARIFY JELLY.

The white of egg is, perhaps, the best substance that can be employed in clarifying jelly, as well as some other fluids, for the reason that when albumen (and the white of egg is nearly pure albumen) is put into a liquid that is muddy, from substances suspended in it, on boiling coagulates in a flocculent manner, and, entangling with the impurities, rises with them to the surface as a scum, or sinks to the bottom, according to their weight.

CONFECTIONERY

In the making of confections the best *granulated* or *loaf* sugar should be used. (Beware of glucose mixed with sugar.) Sugar is boiled more or less, according to the kind of candy to be made, and it is necessary to understand the proper degree of sugar boiling to operate it successfully.

Occasionally sugar made into candies, "creams" or syrups, will need clarifying. The process is as follows: Beat up well the white of an egg with a cupful of cold water and pour it into a very clean iron or thick new tin saucepan, and put into the pan four cupfuls of sugar, mixed with a cupful of warm water. Put on the stove and heat *moderately* until the scum rises. Remove the pan, and skim off the top, then place on the fire again until the scum rises again. Then remove as before, and so continue until no scum rises.

This recipe is good for brown or yellowish sugar; for soft, white sugars, half the white of an egg will do, and for refined or loaf sugar a quarter will do.

The quantities of sugar and water are the same in all cases. Loaf sugar will generally do for all candy-making without further clarification. Brown or yellow sugars are used for caramels, dark-colored cocoanut, taffy, and pulled molasses candies generally.

Havana is the cheapest grade of white sugar and a shade or two lighter than the brown.

Confectioners' A is superior in color and grain to the Havana. It is a centrifugal sugar—that is, it is not re-boiled to procure its white color, but is moistened with water and then put into rapidly-revolving cylinders. The uncrystalized syrup or molasses is whirled out of it, and the sugar comes out with a dry, white grain.

ICING OR POWDERED SUGARS.—This is powdered loaf sugar. Icing can only be made with powdered sugar which is produced by grinding or crushing loaf sugar nearly as fine as flour.

GRANULATED SUGAR—This is a coarse-grained sugar, generally very clean and sparkling, and fit for use as a colored sugar in crystallized goods, and other superior uses.

This same syrup answers for most candies and should be boiled to such a degree, that when a fork or splinter is dipped into it the liquid will run off and form a thick drop on the end, and long silk-like threads hang from it when exposed to the air. The syrup never to be stirred while hot, or else it will grain, but if intended for soft, French candies, should be removed, and, when nearly cold, stirred to a cream. For hard, brittle candies, the syrup should be boiled until, when a little is dropped in *cold* water, it will crack and break when biting it.

The hands should be buttered when handling it, or it will stick to them.

The top of the inside of the dish that the sugar or molasses is to be cooked in should be buttered a few inches around the inside; it prevents the syrup from rising and swelling any higher than where it reaches the buttered edge.

For common crack candies, the sugar can be kept from graining by adding a teaspoonful of vinegar or cream of tartar.

Colorings for candies should be harmless, and those used for fruit and confectionery, on page 444, will be most suitable.

Essences and extracts should be bought at the druggist's, not the poor kind usually sold at the grocer's.

FRENCH CREAM CANDY.

Put four cupfuls of white sugar and one cupful of water into a bright tin pan on the range and let it boil without stirring for ten minutes. If it looks somewhat thick, test it by letting some drop from the spoon, and if it threads, remove the pan to the table. Take out a small spoonful, and rub it against the side of a cake bowl; if it becomes creamy, and will roll into a ball between the fingers, pour the whole into the bowl. When cool enough to bear your finger in it, take it in your lap, stir or beat it with a large spoon, or pudding-stick. It will soon begin to look like cream, and then grow stiffer until you find it necessary to take your hands and work it like bread dough. If it is not boiled enough to cream, set it back upon the range and let it remain one or two minutes, or as long as is necessary, taking care not to cook it too much. Add the flavoring as soon as it begins to cool. This is the foundation of all French creams. It can be made into rolls, and sliced off, or packed in plates and cut into small cubes, or made into any shape imitating French candies. A pretty form is made by coloring some of the cream pink, taking a piece about as large as a hazel nut, and crowding an almond meat half way into one side, till it looks like a bursting kernel. In working, should the cream get too cold, warm it.

To be successful in making this cream, several points are to be remembered; when the boiled sugar is cool enough to beat, if it looks rough and has turned to sugar, it is because it has been boiled *too much*, or has been *stirred*. If, after it is beaten, it does not look like lard or thick cream, and is sandy or sugary instead, it is because you did not let it get cool enough before beating.

It is not boiled enough if it does not harden so as to work like dough, and should not stick to the hands; in this case put it back into the pan with an ounce of hot water, and cook over just enough, by testing in water as above. After it is turned into the bowl to cool, it should look clear as jelly. Practice and patience will make perfect.

FRUIT CREAMS.

Add to "French Cream" raisins, currants, figs, a little citron, chopped and mixed thoroughly through the cream while quite warm. Make into bars or flat cakes.

WALNUT CREAMS.

Take a piece of "French Cream" the size of a walnut. Having cracked some English walnuts, using care not to break the meats, place one-half of each nut upon each side of the ball, pressing them into the ball.

Walnut creams can be made by another method: First take a piece of "French Cream," put it into a cup and setting the cup into a vessel of boiling water, heating it until it turns like thick cream; drop the walnut meats into it, one at a time, taking them out on the end of a fork and placing on buttered paper; continue to dip them until all are used, then go over again, giving them a second coat of candy. They look nice colored pink and flavored with vanilla.

CHOCOLATE CREAMS.

Use "French Cream," and form it into small cone-shaped balls with the fingers. Lay them upon paper to harden until all are formed. Melt one cake of Baker's chocolate in an earthen dish or small basin; by setting it in the oven it will soon melt; do not let it cook, but it *must* be kept *hot*.

Take the balls of cream, one at a time, on the tines of a fork, pour the melted chocolate over them with a teaspoon and when well covered, slip them from the fork upon oiled paper.

COCOANUT CREAMS.

Take two tablespoonfuls of grated cocoanut and half as much "French candy;" work them both together with your hand till the cocoanut is all well mixed in it. If you choose, you can add a drop of vanilla. If too soft to work into balls, add confectioners' sugar to stiffen; make into balls the size of hazelnuts and dip twice, as in the foregoing recipes, flavoring the melted "French Cream" with vanilla.

VARIEGATED CREAMS.

Make the "French Cream" recipe, and divide into three parts, leaving one part white, color one pink with cochineal syrup, and the third part color brown with chocolate, which is done by just letting the cream soften and stirring in a little finely grated chocolate. The pink is colored by dropping on a few drops of cochineal syrup while the cream is warm and beating it in. Take the white cream, make a flat ball of it, and lay it upon a buttered dish, and pat it out flat until about half an inch thick. If it does not work easily, dip the hand in alcohol. Take the pink cream, work in the same way as the white and lay it upon the white; then the chocolate in the same manner, and lay upon the pink, pressing all together. Trim the edges off smooth, leaving it in a nice, square cake, then cut into slices or small cubes, as you prefer. It is necessary to work it all up as rapidly as possible.

RASPBERRY CREAMS.

Stir enough confectioners' sugar into a teaspoonful of raspberry jam to form a thick paste; roll it into balls between the palms of your hands. Put a lump of "French Cream" into a teacup and set it into a basin of boiling water, stirring it until it has melted; then drop a few drops of cochineal coloring to make it a pale pink, or a few drops of raspberry juice, being careful not to add enough to prevent its hardening. Now dip these little balls into the sugar cream, giving them two coats. Lay aside to harden.

Remember to *keep stirring* the melted cream, or if not it will *turn back to clear syrup*.

NUT CREAMS.

Chop almonds, hickory nuts, butternuts or English walnuts quite fine. Make the "'French Cream," and before adding all the sugar, while the cream is quite soft, stir into it the nuts, and then form into balls, bars or squares. Several kinds of nuts may be mixed together.

MAPLE SUGAR CREAMS.

Grate fine maple sugar and mix, in quantity to suit the taste, with "French Cream;" make any shape desired. Walnut creams are sometimes made with maple sugar and are very fine.

STICK CANDY.

One pound of granulated sugar, one cupful of water, a quarter of a cupful of vinegar, or half a teaspoonful of cream of tartar, one small tablespoonful of glycerine. Flavor with vanilla, rose or lemon. Boil all except the flavoring, without stirring, twenty minutes or half an hour, or until crisp when dropped in water. Just before pouring upon greased platters to cool, add half a teaspoonful of soda. After pouring upon platters to cool, pour two teaspoonfuls of flavoring over the top. When partly cool, pull it until very white. Draw it into sticks the size you wish, and cut off with shears into sticks or kiss-shaped drops. It may be colored if desired. (See page 444, for coloring.)

CHOCOLATE CARAMELS.

One cupful of grated chocolate, two cupfuls of brown sugar, one cupful of West India molasses, one cupful of milk or cream, butter the size of an egg, boil until thick, *almost* brittle, stirring constantly. Turn it out on to buttered plates, and when it begins to stiffen, mark it in small squares so that it will break easily when cold. Some like it flavored with a tablespoonful of vanilla.

GRILLED ALMONDS.

These are a very delicious candy seldom met with out of France. They are rather more trouble to make than other kinds, but well repay it from their novel flavor. Blanch a cupful of almonds; dry them thoroughly. Boil a cupful of sugar and a quarter of a cupful of water till it "hairs," then throw in the almonds; let them fry, as it were, in this syrup, stirring them occasionally; they will turn a faint yellow brown before the sugar changes color; do not wait an instant once this change of color begins, or they will lose flavor; remove them from the fire, and stir them until the syrup has turned back to sugar and clings irregularly to the nuts.

These are grilled almonds. You will find them delicious, as they are to alternate at dinner with the salted almonds now so fashionable.

PEPPERMINT DROPS.

One cupful of sugar crushed fine, and just moistened with boiling water, then boiled five minutes; then take from the fire and add cream of tartar the size of a pea; mix well and add four or five drops of oil of peppermint. Beat briskly until the mixture whitens, then drop quickly upon white paper. Have the cream of tartar and oil of peppermint measured while the sugar is boiling. If it sugars before it is all dropped, add a little water and boil a minute or two.

CURRANT DROPS.

Use currant juice instead of water, to moisten a quantity of sugar. Put it in a pan and heat, stirring constantly: be sure not to let it boil; then mix a very little more sugar, let it warm with the rest a moment, then, with a smooth stick, drop on paper.

LEMON DROPS.

Upon a coffeecupful of finely powdered sugar pour just enough lemon juice to dissolve it, and boil it to the consistency of thick syrup, and so that it appears brittle when dropped in cold water. Drop this on buttered plates in drops; set away to cool and harden.

NUT MOLASSES CANDY.

When making molasses candy, add any kind of nuts you fancy; put them in after the syrup has thickened and is ready to take from the fire; pour out on buttered tins. Mark it off in squares before it gets too cool. Peanuts should be fresh roasted and then tossed in a sieve, to free them of their inner skins.

SUGAR NUT CANDY.

Three pounds of white sugar, half a pint of water, half a pint of vinegar, a quarter of a pound of butter, one pound of hickory nut kernels. Put the sugar, butter, vinegar and water together into a thick saucepan. When it begins to thicken, add the nuts. To test it, take up a very small quantity as quickly as possible directly from the centre, taking care not to disturb it any more than is necessary. Drop it into cold water, and remove from the fire the moment the little particles are brittle. Pour into buttered plates. Use any nuts with this recipe.

COCOANUT CANDY.

One cocoanut, one and one-half pounds of granulated sugar. Put sugar and milk of cocoanut together, beat slowly until the sugar is melted, then boil five minutes; add cocoanut (finely grated), boil ten minutes longer, stir constantly to keep from burning. Pour on buttered plates; cut in squares. Will take about two days to harden. Use prepared cocoanut when other cannot be had.

BUTTER-SCOTCH.

Three cupfuls of white sugar, half a cupful of water, half a cupful of vinegar, or half a teaspoonful of cream of tartar, a tablespoonful of butter and eight drops of extract of lemon. Boil *without stirring* till it will snap and break. Just before taking from the fire, add a quarter of a teaspoonful of soda; pour into well-buttered biscuit tins, a quarter of an inch thick. Mark off into inch squares when partly cold.

EVERTON TAFFY, OR BUTTER-SCOTCH.

Two cupfuls of sugar, two cupfuls of dark molasses, one cupful of cold butter, grated rind of half a lemon. Boil over a slow fire until it hardens when dropped in cold water. Pour thinly into tins well buttered, and mark into inch squares before it cools.

MAPLE WALNUTS.

Beat the white of one egg to a stiff froth, stir in enough powdered sugar to make it like hard frosting, dip the walnut meats (which you have taken care to remove from the shells without breaking) in a syrup made by boiling for two or three minutes two tablespoonfuls of maple sugar in one of water, or in this proportion. Press some of the hard frosting between the two halves of the walnut and let it harden. Dates may be prepared in this way, and butternuts and English walnuts also.

POP-CORN CANDY. No. 1.

Put into an iron kettle one tablespoonful of butter, three tablespoonfuls of water and one cupful of white sugar; boil until ready to candy, then throw in three quarts nicely popped corn; stir vigorously until the sugar is evenly distributed over the corn; take the kettle from the fire and stir until it cools a little, and in this way you may have each kernel separate and all coated with the sugar. Of course it must have your undivided attention from the first, to prevent scorching. Almonds, English walnuts, or, in fact, any nuts are delicious prepared in this way.

POP-CORN CANDY. No. 2.

Having popped your corn, salt it and keep it warm, sprinkle over with a whisk broom a mixture composed of an ounce of gum arabic and a half pound of sugar, dissolved in two quarts of water; boil all a few minutes. Stir the corn with the hands or large spoon thoroughly; then mold into balls with the hands.

POP-CORN BALLS.

Take three large ears of pop-corn (rice is best). After popping, shake it down in pan so the unpopped corn will settle at the bottom; put the nice white popped in a greased pan. For the candy, take one cup of molasses, one cup of light brown or white sugar, one tablespoonful of vinegar. Boil until it will harden in water. Pour on the corn. Stir with a spoon until thoroughly mixed; then mold into balls with the hand.

No flavor should be added to this mixture, as the excellence of this commodity depends entirely upon the united flavor of the corn, salt and the sugar or molasses.

HOARHOUND CANDY.

Boil two ounces of dried hoarhound in a pint and a half of water for about half an hour; strain and add three and a half pounds of brown sugar; boil over a hot fire until sufficiently hard; pour out in flat, well-greased tins and mark into sticks or small squares with a knife as soon as cool enough to retain its shape.

JUJUBE PASTE.

Two cupfuls of sugar, one-quarter of a pound of gum arabic, one pint of water. Flavor with the essence of lemon and a grain of cochineal. Let the mixture stand, until the gum is dissolved, in a warm place on the back of the stove, then draw forward and cook until thick; try in cold water; it should be limber and bend when cold. Pour in buttered pans, an eighth of an inch thick; when cool, roll up in a scroll.

CANDIED ORANGES.

Candied orange is a great delicacy, which is easily made: Peel and quarter the oranges; make a syrup in the proportion of one pound of sugar to one pint of water; let it boil until it will harden in water; then take it from the fire and dip the quarters of orange in the syrup; let them drain on a fine sieve placed over a platter so that the syrup will not be wasted; let them drain thus until cool, when the sugar will crystallize. These are nice served with the last course of dinner. Any fruit the same.

FIG CANDY.

One cup of sugar, one-third cup of water, one-fourth teaspoonful cream of tartar. Do not stir while boiling. Boil to amber color, stir in the cream of tartar just before taking from the fire. Wash the figs, open and lay in a tin pan and pour the candy over them. Or you may dip them in the syrup the same as "Candied Oranges."

CANDY ROLEY POLEY.

Take half a pint of citron, half a pint of raisins, half a pound of figs, a quarter of a pound of shelled almonds, one pint of peanuts before they are hulled; cut up the citron, stone the raisins, blanch the almonds, and hull the peanuts; cut up the figs into small bits. Take two pounds of coffee-sugar and moisten with vinegar; put in a piece of butter as large as a walnut; stew till it hardens, but take off before it gets to the brittle stage; beat it with a spoon six or eight times, then stir in the mixed fruits and nuts. Pour into a wet cloth and roll it up like a pudding, twisting the ends of the cloth to mold it. Let it get cold and slice off pieces as it may be wanted for eating.

MOLASSES CANDY.

Put one quart of West India molasses, one cupful of brown sugar, a piece of butter the size of half an egg, into a six-quart kettle. Let it boil over a slack fire until it begins to look thick, stirring it often to prevent burning. Test it by taking some out and dropping a few drops in a cup of cold water. If it hardens quickly and breaks short between the teeth it is boiled enough. Now put in half a teaspoonful of baking soda, and stir it well; then pour it out into well-buttered flat tins. When partly cooled, take up the candy with your hands well buttered then pull and double, and so on, until the candy is a whitish yellow. It may be cut in strips and rolled or twisted.

If flavoring is desired, drop the flavoring on the top as it begins to cool and when it is pulled, the whole will be flavored.

STRAWBERRY CONSERVE.

Prepare the fruit as for preserving, allowing half a pound of loaf sugar to one pound of fruit. Sprinkle the sugar over the fruit at night; in the morning, put it on the fire in a kettle and boil until the berries are clear. Spread on dishes and put in the sun until dry; after which roll the fruit in sugar and pack in jars.

PEACH CONSERVE.

Halve the peaches and take out the stones; pare. Have ready some powdered white sugar on a plate or dish. Roll the peaches in it several times, until they will not take up any more. Place them singly on a plate, with the cup or hollow side up, that the juices may not run out. Lay them in the sun. The next morning roll them again. As soon as the juice seems set in the peaches, turn the other side to the sun. When they are thoroughly dry, pack them in glass jars, or, what is still nicer, fig-drums. They make an excellent sweetmeat just as they are; or, if wanted for table use, put over the fire in porcelain, with a very little water, and stew a few minutes.

PEACH LEATHER.

Stew as many peaches as you choose, allowing a quarter of a pound of sugar to one of fruit; mash it up smooth as it cooks, and when it is dry enough to spread in a thin sheet on a board greased with butter, set it out in the sun to dry; when dry it can be rolled up like leather, wrapped up in a cloth, and will keep perfectly from season to season. School-children regard it as a delightful addition to their lunch of biscuit or cold bread. Apple and quince leather are made in the same fashion, only a little flavoring or spice is added to them.

COCOANUT CARAMELS.

Two cupfuls of grated cocoanut, one cupful of sugar, two tablespoonfuls of flour, the whites of three eggs, beaten stiff. Soak the cocoanut, if desiccated, in milk enough to cover it; then beat the whites of the eggs, add gradually the sugar, cocoanut and flour; with your fingers make, by rolling the mixture, into cone shapes. Place them on buttered sheets of tin covered with buttered letter paper and bake in a moderate heat about fifteen or twenty minutes. They should cool before removing from the tins.

DRIED PRESERVES.

Any of the fruits that have been preserved in syrup may be converted into dry preserves, by first draining them from the syrup and then drying them slowly on the stove, strewing them thickly with powdered sugar. They should be turned every few hours, sifting over them more sugar.

CANDIES WITHOUT COOKING.

Very many candies made by confectioners are made without boiling, which makes them very desirable, and they are equal to the best "French Creams." The secret lies in the sugar used, which is the **XXX** powdered or confectioners' sugar. Ordinary powdered sugar, when rubbed between the thumb and finger has a decided grain, but the confectioners' sugar is fine as flour. The candies made after this process are better the day after.

FRENCH VANILLA CREAM.

Break into a bowl the whites of one or more eggs, as the quantity you wish to make will require; add to it an equal quantity of cold water, then stir in XXX powdered or confectioners' sugar until you have it stiff enough to mold into shape with the fingers. Flavor with vanilla to taste. After it is formed in balls, cubes or lozenge shapes, lay them upon plates or waxed paper and set them aside to dry. This cream can be worked in candies similar to the French cooked cream.

CHOCOLATE CREAM DROPS.

These are made or molded into cone-shape forms with the fingers, from the uncooked "French Cream," similar to that which is cooked. After forming into these little balls or cones, lay them on oiled paper until the next day, to harden, or make them in the morning and leave them until afternoon. Then melt some chocolate (the best confectioners') in a basin set in another basin of boiling water; when melted, and the creams are hard enough to handle, take one at a time on a fork and drop into the melted chocolate, roll it until well covered, then slip from the fork upon oiled or waxed paper, and set them aside to harden.

FRUIT AND NUT CREAMS.

Raisins seeded, currants, figs and citron, chopped fine, and mixed with the uncooked "French Cream," while soft, before the sugar is all mixed in, makes a delicious variety. Nuts also may be mixed with this cream, stirring into it chopped almonds, hickory nuts, butternuts, or English walnuts, then forming them into balls, bars or squares. Several kinds of nuts may be mixed together.

ORANGE DROPS.

Grate the rind of one orange and squeeze the juice, taking care to reject the seeds; add to this a pinch of tartaric acid; then stir in confectioners' sugar until it is stiff enough to form into balls the size of a small marble. This is delicious candy.

The same process for lemon drops, using lemons in place of orange. Color a faint yellow.

COCOANUT CREAMS.

Make the uncooked cream as in the foregoing recipe. Take the cream while soft, add fresh grated cocoanut to taste; add sufficient confectioners' sugar to mold into balls and then roll the balls in the fresh grated cocoanut. These may be colored pink with a few drops of cochineal syrup, also brown by adding a few spoonfuls of grated chocolate; then rolling them in grated cocoanut; the three colors are very pretty together. The coconut cream may be made into a flat cake and cut into squares or strips.

With this uncooked cream, all the recipes given for the cooked "French Cream," may be used: English walnut creams, variegated creams, etc.

COFFEE, TEA, BEVERAGES.

Boiling water is a very important desideratum in the making of a cup of good coffee or tea, but the average housewife is very apt to overlook this fact. Do not boil the water more than three or four minutes; longer boiling ruins the water for coffee or tea making, as most of its natural properties escape by evaporation, leaving a very insipid liquid composed mostly of lime and iron, that would ruin the best coffee, and give the tea a dark, dead look, which ought to be the reverse.

Water left in the tea-kettle over night *must never be used for preparing the breakfast coffee*; no matter how excellent your coffee or tea may be, it will be ruined by the addition of water that has been boiled more than once.

THE HEALING PROPERTIES OF TEA AND COFFEE.

The medical properties of these two beverages are considerable. Tea is used advantageously in inflammatory diseases and as a cure for the headache. Coffee is supposed to act as a preventative of gravel and gout, and to its influence is ascribed the rarity of those diseases in Prance and Turkey. Both tea and coffee powerfully counteract the effects of opium and intoxicating liquors: though, when taken in excess, and without nourishing food, they themselves produce, temporarily at least, some of the more disagreeable consequences incident to the use of ardent spirits. In general, however, none but persons possessing great mobility of the nervous system, or enfeebled or effeminate constitutions, are injuriously affected by the moderate use of tea and coffee in connection with food.

COFFEE.

One full coffeecupful of ground coffee, stirred with one egg and part of the shell, adding a half cupful of *cold* water. Put it into the coffee boiler, and pour on to it a quart of boiling water; as it rises and begins to boil, stir it down with a silver spoon or fork. Boil hard for ten or twelve minutes. Remove from the fire and pour out a cupful of coffee, then pour back into the coffeepot. Place it on the back of the stove or range where it will keep hot (and not boil); it will settle in about five minutes. Send to the table *hot*. Serve with good cream and lump sugar. Three-quarters of a pound of Java and a quarter of a pound of Mocha make the best mixture of coffee.

VIENNA COFFEE.

Equal parts of Mocha and Java coffee; allow one heaping tablespoonful of coffee to each person and two extra to make good strength. Mix one egg with grounds; pour on coffee half as much boiling water as will be needed; let it froth, then stir down grounds, and let boil five minutes; then let it stand where it will keep hot, but not boil, for five or ten minutes, and add rest of water. To one pint of cream add the white of an egg, well beaten; this is to be put in cups with sugar, and hot coffee added.

FILTERED OR DRIP COFFEE.

For each person allow a large tablespoonful of finely ground coffee, and to every tablespoonful allow a cupful of boiling water; the coffee to be one part Mocha to two of Java.

Have a small iron ring made to fit the top of the coffeepot inside, and to this ring sew a small muslin bag (the muslin for the purpose must not be too thin). Fit the bag into the pot, pour some boiling water in it, and, when the pot is well warmed, put the ground coffee into the bag; pour over as much boiling water as is required, close the lid, and, when all the water has filtered through, remove the bag, and send the coffee to table. Making it in this manner prevents the necessity of pouring the coffee from one vessel to another, which cools and spoils it. The water should be poured on the coffee gradually so that the infusion may be stronger; and the bag must be well made that none of the grounds may escape through the seams and so make the coffee thick and muddy.

Patented coffeepots on this principle can be purchased at most house-furnishing stores.

ICED COFFEE.

Make more coffee than usual at breakfast time and stronger. When cold put on ice. Serve with cracked ice in each tumbler.

SUBSTITUTE FOR CREAM IN COFFEE.

Beat the white of an egg, put to it a small lump of butter and pour the coffee into it gradually, stirring it so that it will not curdle. It is difficult to distinguish this from fresh cream.

Many drop a tiny piece of sweet butter into their cup of hot coffee as a substitute for cream.

TO MAKE TEA.

Allow two teaspoonfuls of tea to one large cupful of boiling water. Scald the teapot, put in the tea, pour on about a cupful of *boiling* water, set it on the fire in a warm place, where it will not boil, but keep very hot, to almost boiling; let it steep or "draw" ten or twelve minutes. Now fill up with as much boiling water as is required. Send *hot* to the table. It is better to use a china or porcelain teapot, but if you do use metal let it be tin, new, bright and clean; never use it when the tin is worn off and the iron exposed. If you do you are drinking tea-ate of iron.

To make tea to perfection, boiling water must be poured on the leaves directly it boils. Water which has been boiling more than five minutes, or which has previously boiled, should on no account be used. If the water does not boil, or if it be allowed to overboil, the leaves of the tea will be only half-opened and the tea itself will be quite spoiled. The water should be allowed to remain on the leaves from ten to fifteen minutes.

A Chinese being interviewed for the *Cook* says: Drink your tea plain. Don't add milk or sugar. Tea-brokers and tea-tasters never do; epicures never do; the Chinese never do. Milk contains fibrin, albumen or some other stuff, and the tea a delicate amount of tannin. Mixing the two makes the liquid turbid. This turbidity, if I remember the cyclopædia aright, is tannate of fibrin, or leather. People who put milk in tea are therefore drinking boots and shoes in mild disguise.

ICED TEA.

Is now served to a considerable extent during the summer months. It is of course used without milk, and the addition of sugar serves only to destroy the finer tea flavor. It may be prepared some hours in advance, and should be made stronger than when served hot. It is bottled and placed in the ice chest till required. Use the black or green teas, or both, mixed, as fancied.

CHOCOLATE.

Allow half a cupful of grated chocolate to a pint of water and a pint of milk. Rub the chocolate smooth in a little cold water and stir into the boiling water. Boil twenty minutes, add the milk and boil ten minutes more, stirring it often. Sweeten to your taste.

The French put two cupfuls of boiling water to each cupful of chocolate. They throw in the chocolate just as the water commences to boil. Stir it with a spoon as soon as it boils up, add two cupfuls of good milk, and when it has boiled sufficiently, serve a spoonful of thick whipped cream with each cup.

COCOA.

Six tablespoonfuls of cocoa to each pint of water, as much milk as water, sugar to taste. Rub cocoa smooth in a little cold water; have ready on the fire a pint of boiling water; stir in grated cocoa paste. Boil twenty minutes, add milk and boil five minutes more, stirring often. Sweeten in cups so as to suit different tastes.

BUTTERMILK AS A DRINK.

Buttermilk, so generally regarded as a waste product, has latterly been coming somewhat into vogue, not only as a nutrient, but as a therapeutic agent, and in an editorial article the *Canada Lancet*, some time ago, highly extolled its virtues. Buttermilk may be roughly described as milk which has lost most of its fat and a small percentage of casein, and which has become sour by fermentation. Long experience has demonstrated it to be an agent of superior digestibility. It is, indeed, a true milk peptone—that is, milk already partly digested, the coagulation of the coagulable portion being loose and flaky, and not of that firm indigestible nature which is the result of the action of the gastric juice upon cow's sweet milk. It resembles koumiss in its nature, and, with the exception of that article, it is the most grateful, refreshing and digestible of the products of milk. It is a decided laxative to the bowels, a fact which must be borne in mind in the treatment of typhoid fever, and which may be turned to advantage in the treatment of habitual constipation. It is a diuretic, and may be prescribed with advantage in some kidney troubles. Owing to its acidity, combined with its laxative properties, it is believed to exercise a general impression on the liver. It is well adapted to many cases where it is customary to recommend lime water and milk. It is invaluable in the treatment of diabetes, either exclusively, or alternating with skimmed milk. In some cases of gastric ulcer and cancer of the stomach, it is the only food that can be retained.

Medical journal.

CURRANT WINE. No. 1.

The currants should be quite ripe. Stem, mash and strain them, adding a half pint of water and less than a pound of sugar to a quart of the mashed fruit.

Stir well up together and pour into a clean cask, leaving the bung-hole open, or covered with a piece of lace. It should stand for a month to ferment, when it will be ready for bottling; just before bottling you may add a small quantity of brandy or whisky.

CURRANT WINE. No. 2.

To each quart of currant juice, add two quarts of soft water and three pounds of brown sugar. Put into a jug or small keg, leaving the top open until fermentation ceases and it looks clear. Draw off and cork tightly.

Long Island Recipe.

BLACKBERRY WINE. No. 1.

Cover your blackberries with cold water; crush the berries well with a wooden masher; let them stand twenty-four hours; then strain, and to one gallon of juice put three pounds of common brown sugar; put into wide-mouthed jars for several days, carefully skimming off the scum that will rise to the top; put in several sheets of brown paper and let them remain in it three days; then skim again and pour through a funnel into your cask. There let it remain undisturbed till March; then strain again and bottle. These directions, if carefully followed out, will insure you excellent wine.

Orange County Recipe.

BLACKBERRY WINE NO. 2

Berries should be ripe and plump. Put into a large wood or stone vessel with a tap; pour on sufficient boiling water to cover them; when cool enough to bear your hand, bruise well until all the berries are broken; cover up, let stand until berries begin to rise to top, which will occur in three or four days. Then draw off the clear juice in another vessel, and add one pound of sugar to every ten quarts of the liquor, and stir thoroughly. Let stand six to ten days in first vessel with top; then draw off through a jelly-bag. Steep four ounces of isinglass in a pint of wine for twelve hours; boil it over a slow fire till all dissolved, then place dissolved isinglass in a gallon of blackberry juice, give them a boil together and pour all into the vessel. Let stand a few days to ferment and settle; draw off and keep in a cool place. Other berry wines may be made in the same manner.

GRAPE WINE.

Mash the grapes and strain them through a cloth; put the skins in a tub, after squeezing them, with barely enough water to cover them; strain the juice thus obtained into the first portion; put three pounds of sugar to one gallon of the mixture; let it stand in an open tub to ferment, covered with a cloth, for a period of from three to seven days; skim off what rises every morning. Put the juice in a cask and leave it open for twenty-four hours; then bung it up, and put clay over the bung to keep the air out. Let your wine remain in the cask until March, when it should be drawn off and bottled.

FLORIDA ORANGE WINE.

Wipe the oranges with a wet cloth, peel off the yellow rind very thin, squeeze the oranges, and strain the juice through a hair-sieve; measure the juice after it is strained and for each gallon allow three pounds of granulated sugar, the white and shell of one egg and one-third of a gallon of cold water; put the sugar, the white and shell of the egg (crushed small) and the water over the fire and stir them every two minutes until the eggs begin to harden; then boil the syrup until it looks clear under the froth, of egg which will form on the surface; strain the syrup, pour it upon the orange rind and let it stand over night; then next add the orange juice and again let it stand over night; strain it the second day, and put it into a tight cask with a small cake of compressed yeast to about ten gallons of wine, and leave the bung out of the cask until the wine ceases to ferment; the hissing noise continues so long as fermentation is in progress; when fermentation ceases, close the cask by driving in the bung, and let the wine stand about nine months before bottling it; three months after it is bottled, it can be used. A glass of brandy added to each gallon of wine after fermentation ceases is generally considered an improvement.

There are seasons of the year when Florida oranges by the box are very cheap, and this fine wine can be made at a small expense.

METHELIN, OR HONEY WINE.

This is a very ancient and popular drink in the north of Europe. To some new honey, strained, add spring water; put a whole egg into it; boil this liquor till the egg swims above the liquor; strain, pour it in a cask. To every fifteen gallons add two ounces of white Jamaica ginger, bruised, one ounce of cloves and mace, one and one-half ounces of cinnamon, all bruised together and tied up in a muslin bag; accelerate the fermentation with yeast; when worked sufficiently, bung up; in six weeks draw off into bottles.

Another Mead.—Boil the combs, from which the honey has been drained, with sufficient water to make a tolerably sweet liquor; ferment this with yeast and proceed as per previous formula.

Sack Mead is made by adding a handful of hops and sufficient brandy to the comb liquor.

BLACK CURRANT WINE.

Four quarts of whisky, four quarts of black currants, four pounds of brown or white sugar, one tablespoonful of cloves, one tablespoonful of cinnamon.

Crush the currants and let them stand in the whisky with the spices for three weeks; then strain and add the sugar; set away again for three weeks longer; then strain and bottle.

RAISIN WINE.

Take two pounds of raisins, seed and chop them, a lemon, a pound of white sugar and about two gallons of boiling water. Pour into a stone jar and stir daily for six or eight days. Strain, bottle and put in a cool place for ten days or so, when the wine will be ready for use.

CHERRY BOUNCE.

To one gallon of wild cherries add enough good whisky to cover the fruit. Let soak two or three weeks and then drain off the liquor. Mash the cherries without breaking the stones and strain through a jelly-bag; add this liquor to that already drained off. Make a with a gill of water and a pound of white sugar to every two of liquor thus prepared; stir in well and bottle, and tightly cork. A common way of making cherry bounce is to put wild cherries and whisky together in a jug and use the liquor as wanted.

BLACKBERRY CORDIAL.

Warm and squeeze the berries; add to one pint of juice one pound of white sugar, one-half ounce of powdered cinnamon, one-fourth ounce of mace, two teaspoonfuls of cloves. Boil all together for one-fourth of an hour; strain the syrup, and to each pint add a glass of French brandy. Two or three doses of a tablespoonful or less will check any slight diarrhoea. When the attack is violent, give a tablespoonful after each discharge until the complaint is in subjection. It will arrest dysentery if given in season, and is a pleasant and safe remedy. Excellent for children when teething.

HOP BEER.

Take five quarts of water, six ounces of hops, boil it three hours; then strain the liquor, add to it five quarts of water, four ounces of bruised ginger root; boil this again twenty minutes, strain and add four pounds of sugar. When luke-warm put in a pint of yeast. Let it ferment; in twenty-four hours it will be ready for bottling.

GINGER BEER.

Put into a kettle two ounces of powdered ginger root (or more if it is not very strong), half an ounce of cream of tartar, two large lemons, cut in slices, two pounds of broken loaf sugar and two gallons of soft boiling water. Simmer them over a slow fire for half an hour. When the liquor is nearly cold, stir into it a large tablespoonful of the best yeast. After it has fermented, which will be in about twenty-four hours, bottle for use.

SPRUCE BEER.

Allow an ounce of hops and a spoonful of ginger to a gallon of water. When well boiled, strain it and put in a pint of molasses, or a pound of brown sugar, and half an ounce or less of the essence of spruce; when cool, add a teacupful of yeast, and put into a clean tight cask, and let it ferment for a day or two, then bottle it for use. You can boil the sprigs of spruce fir in place of the essence.

ROMAN PUNCH. No. 1.

Grate the yellow rind of four lemons and two oranges upon two pounds of loaf sugar. Squeeze the juice of the lemons and oranges; cover it and let it stand until next day. Strain it through a sieve, mix with the sugar; add a bottle of champagne and the whites of eight eggs beaten to a stiff froth. It may be frozen or not, as desired. For winter use snow instead of ice.

ROMAN PUNCH. No. 2.

Make two quarts of lemonade, rich with pure juice lemon fruit; add one tablespoonful of extract of lemon. Work well and freeze; just before serving, add for each quart of ice half a pint of brandy and half a pint of Jamaica rum. Mix well and serve in high glasses, as this makes what is called a semi or half ice. It is usually served at dinners as a *coup de milieu*.

DELICIOUS JUNKET.

Take two quarts of new milk, warm it on the stove to about blood heat, pour it into a glass or china bowl and stir into it two tablespoonfuls of prepared rennet, two tablespoonfuls of powdered loaf sugar, and a small wine-glassful of pale brandy. Let it stand till cold and eat with sugar and rich cream. Half the quantity can be made.

RASPBERRY SHRUB.

One quart of raspberry juice, half a pound of loaf sugar, dissolved, a pint of Jamaica rum, or part rum and brandy. Mix thoroughly. Bottle for use.

SASSAFRAS MEAD.

Mix gradually with two quarts of boiling water three pounds and a half of the best brown sugar, a pint and a half of good West India molasses, and a quarter of a pound of tartaric acid. Stir it well and when cool, strain it into a large jug or pan, then mix in a teaspoonful (not more) of essence of sassafras. Transfer it to clean bottles (it will fill about half a dozen), cork it tightly and keep it in a cool place. It will be fit for use next day. Put into a box or boxes a quarter of a pound of carbonate of soda, to use with it. To prepare a glass of sassafras mead for drinking, put a large tablespoonful of the mead into half a tumbler full of ice-water, stir into it a half teaspoonful of the soda and it will immediately foam up to the top.

Sassafras mead will be found a cheap, wholesome and pleasant beverage for warm weather. The essence of sassafras, tartaric acid and carbonate of soda, can, of course, be obtained at the druggist's.

CREAM SODA WITHOUT THE FOUNTAIN.

Coffee-sugar, four pounds, three pints of water, three nutmegs, grated, the whites of ten eggs, well beaten, gum arabic, one ounce, twenty drops of oil of lemon, or extract equal to that amount. By using oils or other fruits, you can make as many flavors from this as you desire. Mix all and place over a gentle fire, and stir well about thirty minutes; remove from the fire and strain, and divide into two parts; into one-half put eight ounces of bicarbonate of soda, into the other half put six ounces of tartaric acid. Shake well, and when cold they are ready for use by pouring three or four spoonfuls from both parts into separate glasses, each one-third full of water. Stir each and pour together, and you have a nice glass of cream soda which you can drink at your leisure, as the gum and eggs hold the gas.

WINE WHEY.

Sweeten one pint of milk to taste, and when boiling, throw in two wine-glasses of sherry; when the curd forms, strain the whey through a muslin bag into tumblers.

LEMON SYRUP.

Take the juice of twelve lemons; grate the rind of six in it, let it stand over night; then take six pounds of white sugar and make a thick syrup. When it is quite cool, strain the juice into it, and squeeze as much oil from the grated rind as will suit the taste. Put in bottles, securely corked, for future use. A tablespoonful in a goblet of water will make a delicious drink on a hot day.

FOR A SUMMER DRAUGHT.

The juice of one lemon, a tumblerful of cold water, pounded sugar to taste, half a small teaspoonful of carbonate of soda. Squeeze the juice from the lemon; strain and add it to the water, with sufficient pounded sugar to sweeten the whole nicely. When well mixed, put in the soda, stir well and drink while the mixture is in an effervescing state.

NOYEAU CORDIAL.

To one gallon of proof spirit add three pounds of loaf sugar and a tablespoonful of extract of almonds. Mix well together and allow to stand forty-eight hours; covered closely; now strain through thick flannel and bottle. This liquor will be much improved by adding half a pint of apricot or peach juice.

EGG NOG.

Beat the yolks of twelve eggs very light, stir in as much white sugar as they will dissolve, pour in gradually one glass of brandy to cook the egg, one glass of old whisky, one grated nutmeg, and three pints of rich milk. Beat the whites to a froth and stir in last.

EGG FLIP, OR MULLED ALE.

Boil one quart of good ale with some nutmeg; beat up six eggs and mix them with a little cold ale; then pour the hot ale to it, pour it back and forth several times to prevent its curdling; warm and stir it till sufficiently thick; add a piece of butter or a glass of brandy and serve it with dry toast.

MILK PUNCH.

One pint of milk made very sweet; a wine-glassful of brandy or rum, well stirred together; grate a little nutmeg over the top of the glasses. Serve with a straw in each glass.

FINE MILK PUNCH.

PARE off the yellow rind of four large lemons and steep it for twenty-four hours in a quart of brandy or rum. Then mix with it the juice of the lemons, a pound and a half of loaf sugar, two grated nutmegs and a quart of water. Add a quart of rich unskimmed milk, made boiling hot, and strain the whole through a jelly-bag. You may either use it as soon as it is cold, or make a larger quantity (in the above proportions) and bottle it. It will keep several months.

TO MAKE HOT PUNCH.

Half a pint of rum, half a pint of brandy, quarter of a pound of sugar, one large lemon, half a teaspoonful of nutmeg, one pint of boiling water.

Rub the sugar over the lemon until it has absorbed all the yellow part of the skin, then put the sugar into a punch bowl; add the lemon juice (free from pips) and mix these two ingredients, well together. Pour over them the boiling water, stir well together, add the rum, brandy and nutmeg; mix thoroughly and the punch will be ready to serve. It is very important in making good punch that all the ingredients are thoroughly incorporated; and to insure success, the processes of mixing must be diligently attended to. (This is an old-style punch.)

LEMONADE.

Three lemons to a pint of water makes strong lemonade; sweeten to your taste.

STRAWBERRY WATER.

Take one cupful of ripe hulled berries; crush with a wooden spoon, mixing with the mass a quarter of a pound of pulverized sugar and half a pint of cold water. Pour the mixture into a fine sieve, rub through and filter till clear; add the strained juice, of one lemon and one and a half pints of cold water, mix thoroughly and set in ice chest till wanted.

This makes a nice, cool drink on a warm day and easily to be made in strawberry season.

STRAWBERRY AND RASPBERRY SYRUP.

Mash the fresh fruit, express the juice and to each quart add three and a half pounds of granulated sugar. The juice, heated to 180° Fahrenheit, and strained or filtered previous to dissolving the sugar, will keep for an indefinite time, canned hot in glass jars.

The juice of soft fruits is best when allowed to drop therefrom by its own weight; lightly mash the fruit and then suspend in a cloth, allowing the juice to drop in a vessel beneath. Many housekeepers, after the bottles and jars are thoroughly washed and dried, smoke them with sulphur in this way: Take a piece of wire and bend it around a small piece of brimstone the size of a bean; set the brimstone on fire, put it in the jar or bottle, bending the other end over the mouth of the vessel, and cover with a cork; after the brimstone has burned away, fill the vessel with the syrup or preserves and cover tightly. There is no sulphurous taste left by the process.

KOUMISS.

Koumiss is prepared by dissolving four ounces of white sugar in one gallon of skimmed milk, and placing in bottles of the capacity of one quart; add two ounces of baker's yeast or a cake of compressed yeast to each bottle. Cork and tie securely, set in a warm place until fermentation is well under way, and lay the bottles on their sides in a cool cellar. In three days, fermentation will have progressed sufficiently to permit the koumiss to be in good condition.

PINEAPPLE VINEGAR.

Cover sliced pineapples with pure cider vinegar; let them stand three or four days, then mash and strain through a cloth as long as it runs clear; to every three quarts of juice add five pounds of sugar.

Boil it altogether about ten minutes, skim carefully until nothing rises to the surface, take from the fire; when cool, bottle it. Blackberries and raspberries, and, in fact, any kind of highly flavored fruit, is fine; a tablespoonful in a glass of ice-cold water, to drink in warm weather.

RASPBERRY VINEGAR. No. 1.

Put a quart of raspberries into a suitable dish, pour over them a quart of good vinegar, let it stand twenty-four hours, then strain through a flannel bag and pour this liquor on another quart of berries; do this for three or four days successively and strain it; make it very sweet with loaf sugar; bottle and seal it.

RASPBERRY VINEGAR. NO. 2.

Turn over a quart or ripe raspberries, mashed, a quart of good cider vinegar, add one pound of white sugar, mix well, then let stand in the sun four hours. Strain it, squeeze out the juice and put in a pint of good brandy. Seal it up in bottles, air-tight, and lay them on their sides in the cellar; cover them with sawdust. When used, pour two tablespoonfuls to a tumblerful of ice-water. Fine.

HOME-MADE TABLE VINEGAR.

Put in an open cask four gallons of warm rain-water, one gallon of common molasses and two quarts of yeast; cover the top with thin muslin and leave it in the sun, covering it up at night and when it rains. In three or four weeks it will be good vinegar. If cider can be used in place of rain-water the vinegar will make much sooner—will not take over a week to make a very sharp vinegar. Excellent for pickling purposes.

VERY STRONG TABLE VINEGAR.

Take two gallons of good cider and thoroughly mix it with two pounds of new honey, pour into your cask or bottle and let it stand from four to six months, when you will have vinegar so strong that it cannot be used at table without diluting with water. It is the best ever procured for pickling purposes.

PINEAPPLE-ADE.

Pare and slice some very ripe pineapples; then cut the slices into small pieces. Put them with all their juice into a large pitcher, and sprinkle among them plenty of powdered white sugar. Pour on boiling water, allowing a small half pint to each pineapple. Cover the pitcher and let it stand till quite cool, occasionally pressing down the pineapple with a spoon. Then set the pitcher for a while in ice. Lastly, strain the infusion into another vessel and transfer it to tumblers, putting into each glass some more sugar and a bit of ice. This beverage will be found delicious.

SEIDLITZ POWDERS.

Fold in a white paper a mixture of one drachm of Rochelle salts and twenty-five grains of carbonate of soda, in a blue paper twenty grains of tartaric acid. They should all be pulverized very finely. Put the contents of the white paper into a tumbler, not quite half full of cold water, and stir it till dissolved. Then put the mixture from the blue paper into another tumbler with the same quantity of water, and stir that also. When the powders are dissolved in both tumblers, pour the first into the other, and it will effervesce immediately. Drink it quickly, while foaming.

INEXPENSIVE DRINK.

A very nice, cheap drink which may take the place of lemonade and be found fully as healthful is made with one cupful of pure cider vinegar, half a cupful of good molasses, put into one quart pitcher of ice-water. A tablespoonful of ground ginger added makes a healthful beverage.

www.ingramcontent.com/pod-product-compliance
Lightning Source LLC
Chambersburg PA
CBHW080615110526
44587CB00040BB/3713